Adoption: STORIES OF LIVES TRANSFORMED

The
Adoption
Exchange
Connecting Children and
Families Since 1983

CELEBRATING 25 YEARS

Adoption: Stories of lives transformed

ADOPTION: Stories of Lives Transformed

Text Copyright © 2008 by Dr. Dixie van de Flier Davis
Book Design by Tanya Haynes, ProComm
Cover Design by Fedra Carina Meredith, Afterhours
Group, Inc.

Send written requests to:
Pie in the Sky Publishing, LLC
8031 East Phillips Circle
Centennial, CO 80112

303-773-0851

www.PieintheSkyPublishing.com

Library of Congress Control Number 2007930755

ISBN 978-1-893815-42-1

First Edition A B C D E

Printed in China

Pie *in the* Sky
PUBLISHING

Aknowledgements

The stories you'll read in this book aren't fabricated in any way. They are about real children, real parents, and real people who care about them. It could not have been written without the generous participation of individuals who courageously opened their lives to tell about their experiences.

Though many of the children and their parents stay in touch with us, over time, most of the children grow up and disappear into the fabric of society, which is exactly what should happen. We have reached back through the past twenty-five years to compile these stories of lives transformed through adoption, and in a few instances we have been unable to reach the family members to talk with them about this book. In those rare instances, we have changed names to preserve their anonymity. Their stories are written as they told them to us, and they were accurate as of the time we were last in touch.

As with everything done by The Adoption Exchange, committee members and numerous supporters selflessly supported and directed the project. Many thanks to Jillian Hochstetler, Sue Hamilton, Madge Walls, Tanya Haynes and Nancy Mills for editing, indexing, design, and publishing. To Alice Weiss Doyel, Elaine Torres, Pam Kiker, Shelbi Perry and David Zinger, thanks for sharing the excitement and giving direction and life to the effort. In the final pages of the book you will find the names of several current and past board members who provided financial support.

It is difficult to select from the thousands of stories to be told, because The Adoption Exchange is indebted to each of the staff members, parents, volunteers, and supporters who have shared our vision for safety and stability for our country's most vulnerable children. Thanks to each of you for encouraging and inspiring us. These are your stories.

Dedication

This book is dedicated to the children
who face their fears and allow themselves to be loved,
and to each of the children who still wait and hope.

Table of Contents

Introduction

Anniversaries are such a special time! In an era in our country when more than half of all marriages fail and only forty-four percent of new businesses survive four years, it is nothing less than remarkable that The Adoption Exchange has survived and thrived for twenty-five years.

This is a success well worth celebrating. It couldn't have happened without devoted staff and contributors, families willing to take risks, and huge community support. Many, many factors and people have contributed to the success of The Adoption Exchange. The purpose of these pages is to share the stories of the children who have found forever families, their

adoptive parents, and the volunteers; so we build on the work of the past twenty-five years and move into the next phase of growth for The Adoption Exchange. The cover of this book features a picture of a leaf with morning dew. The dew is reminiscent of the power to refresh life and bring in positive transformation and growth. Many lives have been transformed by The Adoption Exchange in the past twenty-five years. Mine has certainly been one of them.

I was part of a group of dedicated child welfare advocates who founded The Adoption Exchange in 1983 with a $20,000 challenge grant. The mission grew to include the subsidiary, the *Wednesday's Child* Foundation. Headquartered in Denver, The Adoption

Exchange today maintains offices in Utah, New Mexico, Nevada, and Missouri. In the past twenty-five years The Adoption Exchange has facilitated over 4,556 adoptions for children living in the care of the child welfare system.

Families world-wide and member states of Colorado, Missouri, Nevada, New Mexico, Oklahoma, South Dakota, Utah and Wyoming utilize the broad range of services of The Adoption Exchange to recruit and sustain families for children in foster care. The Adoption Exchange was one of the first U.S. agencies to begin working with institutionalized children and child welfare colleagues in Romania in 1990. It boasts one of the longest-lasting media partnerships (twenty-six years running *Wednesday's Child* weekly on the same major television network news station). The Adoption Exchange now runs *Wednesday's Child* on four major network stations and two Spanish-speaking stations.

I have been privileged to find myself in the company of great national leaders during the course of the past twenty-five years. I was the recipient of the 2007 Child Advocate of the Year Award from the North American Council on Adoptable Children. I have served on numerous expert work groups and national advisory committees of the Departments of Justice and Health & Human Services. I am a founding member and Past President of *Voice for Adoption*, a national advocacy organization. I pioneered the development of a network of collaborating organizations to serve military families and Americans living abroad. For me, it always comes back to the children and their adoptive families.

After twenty-five years with The Adoption Exchange I have learned that love can't change the past. But every day I see it change the future in powerful ways. It changes the one who is loved. And it surely changes the one who loves.

Love enables parents and children to face unexpected challenges when they come together as a new family. It is the bridge that sustains them across the inevitable differences and disappointments.

I've learned that adoption offers both parents and children the opportunity to be all that they ever hoped to become. Hard work, frequent use of therapeutic and educational services, tenacity, commitment, and love are the stuff that raise the child and define the parent.

It is love that induces us to learn and grow - and change when we have to! It is love that propels us to take on the improbable. It is love that inspires us to stretch beyond our own immediate families to adopt, volunteer, or make a sacrificial donation that profoundly changes us and the future.

I learned these lessons in love by listening to children who have survived unspeakable abuses, and by watching their adoptive families. I learned these lessons by working beside hundreds of volunteers, dedicated staff, and board members. I'm thrilled to share their stories with you.

Dr. Dixie van de Flier Davis
President and Executive Director
The Adoption Exchange, Inc.

Hauk; Tatiana, Carlos and Qiana; and Andrew

The Resilience of Human Nature

There is nothing we could do that is more important, or more fullfilling than giving a child a future that includes love, safety and a chance to thrive. Over and over again adopted children and their parents talk about the joys of being a family. You might wonder, then, why we begin our book with a chapter on grief and loss. Often times adoption is rooted in grief and loss and that's where adoption has its beginning. Adoption itself isn't sad. But the circumstances that lead to the need for adoption can break the hearts and wound the spirits of the child, the adoptive parents, and the birth family members. And when we let it, adoption is a process that transforms every one of us who is involved in it. Like all changes in life, the process isn't without pain and loss.

When a child gets a permanent family, that child has already lived the loss of loved ones. It doesn't matter whether that love has been imperfect or harmful. The child loses years of learning, loving, and growing. Innocence and the chance to just be a kid are often the casualties of this hurt. A child's place in a family disappears, and so does the power to access the adults who make life-changing decisions. Judges, adoption supervisors, and caseworkers are frightening strangers that hold the power to his or her future. The child may be separated temporarily or permanently from siblings, aunts, uncles, and grandparents. Friends, school, personal items, and familiarity disappear. The opportunity for the child to try and mend the family one last time is gone. The sense of safety and security disappears. Fear, distrust, and anger take hold.

Children create inventive methods to cope with loss. Raised in foster care, one of our board members remembers convincing herself that her birth mom was a famous movie star who left because she was so very busy. In her little girl's fantasy, the longing and emptiness were masked by a certainty that her mother would return for her, scoop her up, and take her to live in a palatial home.

Children and adults grieve in different ways. Children act out their feelings. Their grieving process is developmental and they will return to the loss from time to time as they grow. Frequent moves while in foster care re-traumatize them and add layers of loss upon loss. Psychotherapists report that grief plays itself out through trouble in school. Dr. Joyce Pavao, Founder and CEO of the Center for Family Connections, describes the struggle of one boy in math, particularly with subtraction. Eventually he told his therapist, "When they say 'take away' I feel so sad."

The children may refuse to remember their own stories and emotionally shut down. An innocent question like "how did you get your pretty name?" creates anxiety. The children never know what will remind them of the loss or when that reminder will catch them by surprise.

The Oklahoma City bombing and 9/11 attacks prompted a serious look at trauma recovery. Researcher and writer, Gail Sheehy articulates in her book *Middletown America* - that there is no such thing as "closure." Terrors come back to haunt them in their nightmares and nag at them at every developmental stage.

The first thing adoptive parents lose when they become clients of the system is a certain sense of individuality. It can feel a little like becoming a military inductee, a hospital patient, or a new employee in a large corporation. They fill out forms, wait for appointments, talk with multiple staff members, and learn the "rules of the game" can be draining.

There is no way to know in advance how their child's issues will challenge their own self-esteem. They arrive at a point where they have to let go of the child they imagined in order to claim the child that is. They imagine what they will be like as parents to an adopted child. Sometimes they find they have to abandon their fantasies of perfection and learn to become parents of the real children they adopt. They expect to rescue a child, to do so much better for this child than others before them. Sometimes their love doesn't seem like it is enough.

As adoptive parents come to love their child and are confronted with the devastating consequences of that child's losses, they are haunted with another kind of grief. "I wish I had been there to be his parent in those first years. I wish I could have protected him from all of those experiences that left these scars."

The sadness may be accompanied by anger and outrage at the circumstances, the perpetrators of pain, and the imperfect child welfare system that didn't always get it right. These things shouldn't happen. Not to anyone. Not to my child.

And what about the birth family? The parents completely lose their relationships with their child, the opportunity to be a parent, and their places in the social order of the community. Grandparents, cousins, uncles, and aunts lose a member of their family. Life-changing circumstances, beyond the control of the birth family, like the illness of a parent, can lead to adoption.

The Adoption Exchange coordinates some of the longest-lasting *Wednesday's Child* television series in the country. Every Wednesday for more than twenty-five years these stations have featured waiting children during their prime-time news broadcasts. When I saw one young boy on this broadcast, I wondered why he had to leave his grandmother. A few months later, rather by chance, I met her and learned that the child's grandmother had to face an unthinkable loss when it became clear that her daughter's mental illness was so severe that she couldn't provide protection and a healthy home for her grandson. Eventually the grandmother, Anna (not her real name)

recognized that it was no longer safe for him to have contact with his mother. Anna's mentally ill daughter had no one else and needed her mother's support and guidance. To protect him, Anna made the heartbreaking choice to let go of her only grandchild. Not surprisingly this little boy had a request of his adoptive parents. "Some day, will you help me find my mommy again?" he asked.

Birth father George Dibble knows the agony of separation. In 2003 he poured out his grief in a song for a son he had recently relinquished to adoption. "Times have been hard as he was born just two weeks ago, and being adopted my emotions are obviously running high. I have never met my birth parents and they have left me no trail on how to find them. So in return I have written a song for the child I have just put up for adoption called *Unknown Son*. …One day if this child comes looking for me I'll know I have at least left him a trail."

During the grieving process unexpected gifts like the ability to make new friends and build new lives become part of recovery. Adoption is a testament to the resilience of human nature. In this chapter George Dibble, Kathy Searle, Nancy and John and Susan Bavaria share their stories on loss.

A Lot Smarter

There is a light out there
It may not be here, but it's somewhere
I may not see it, but I know I need it
Since I've only lived bad,
I don't know what it feels like to be glad
I wish and wish, but I always miss
I want love along with the opportunity to shine like a dove
I want to give up, every day is harder to stand up
I got to keep trying and stop thinking of lying
I'm sick of being used even
though it's better than being abused
You nearly killed me, but slightly skilled me
Thank you, but I still don't hate you

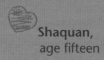

Shaquan,
age fifteen

I Weep for the Memories of My Heart

I weep that no one marveled at the miracle of your birth.

I weep that I missed the sweet smell of your skin after your first bath.

I weep that no one spent hours memorizing the shape of your nose,
the curve of your eyes and the lines in your skin.

I weep that no one remembers your first words.

I weep that smiles and cheers didn't herald after your first step.

I weep that hands didn't mean caring and concern, but pain and confusion.

I weep that when your life should have been filled with exploring the wonders
of the world, it was consumed with finding enough food to stay alive.

I weep that you didn't know the love of grandparents and other adults, but you learned
that no one can be trusted.

I weep that when you woke up early on Saturday mornings,
they weren't filled with watching cartoons, but with waiting and watching
for a mother who only sometimes came back.

I weep that I didn't find you before you gave up hope and closed the window
to your soul in order to survive.

I weep that I can't give up hoping that one day you will be whole.

I weep that I can't replace the last years with the memories of my heart.

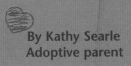

By Kathy Searle
Adoptive parent

A Pocket Full of Miracles

First published in *Heartlines* Spring 2003

Nancy and John met Howard for the first time on Mother's Day in 1984 at his foster home in Cheyenne, Wyoming. The next month Howard moved into their home in Bellevue, Colorado, a suburb of Fort Collins. He was ten-years-old. That first night he had two major seizures, but - because of his parents' faith and persistence - they ended up being his last. *Miracle Number One.*

"When we saw the picture of Howard, we knew immediately this boy was meant to be our child," Nancy said. At the time, Howard had a seizure disorder, was developmentally disabled, and was not expected to live independently.

"Howard was underweight when we first met him, and probably malnourished," Nancy reported. "Once we started him on a nutritious, natural-food diet with supplements, he gained weight quickly and his health improved dramatically. He also was able to go off his seizure medication entirely." *Miracle Number Two.*

Howard's teen years were extraordinarily difficult. The traumatic experiences of his childhood, especially the constant moves through the foster care system, made him feel very angry. Not surprisingly, he had difficulty trusting anyone. When he was fourteen, conflicts at home grew very intense and he began to "act out" violently. At that point, he had to be moved to a group home in Denver where closer supervision and control could be exercised. While this was tremendously painful for his parents, they now believe it was the best thing for them and for Howard. It allowed Howard to develop trust for them on his own terms.

"Over time," Nancy said, "We realized we simply needed to listen, to hear, and to support. When we adopted Howard, it was for life. We let him know that often."

Unsupervised one night, Howard and a friend from the group home went for a walk and attempted to cross a major highway. The boys were struck by a passing car. Howard's friend was killed. Although Howard's legs were broken in the collision, he survived. *Miracle Number Three.*

The loss of his friend was a major turning point for Howard. "He matured through the tragedy," Nancy said. "He started to act like the person I knew he already was. He became a star at the group home, showing a lot more compassion and responsibility toward other members of the group, especially those who were more disabled than he."

Howard graduated from high school while still recovering from the accident. "When they wheeled him across the stage to accept his diploma," Nancy said, "I lost it. There he was, surpassing everyone's wildest expectations." She marvels at the support they've received in raising Howard. "We have 'collected' hundreds of people on our team," she notes, "wonderful, caring people who have helped us and Howard so much over the years."

Today, Howard is thriving. He lives independently in a group home in Fort Collins and holds a steady job. *Miracle Number Four.* He navigates the bus system all over town, does his own grocery shopping and cooking, and is a member of a championship Special Olympics basketball team. *Miracle Number Five.* His parents try to go to every game and cheer louder than anyone else in the stands.

In addition, he often spends weekends with dad doing "guy things." John considers him an important and competent helper, plus a real companion. Two years ago Howard asked to be baptized and his father accompanied him to classes. His parents report that Howard's faith is growing steadily. "Everyone at church tells me how much they think Howard has changed in a short time. He's grown not only physically and socially, but spiritually," John says. *Miracle Number Six.*

"We are experiencing this transition where we can enjoy Howard as a person, not just as our child," Nancy adds. "That is a wonderful thing for any parent."

Unknown Son

Welcome to the world,
Welcome to this place, Little One,
Open up your eyes,
Look the world in the face, Little One,

I wonder what your doing as I speak,
If when your older you'd like to meet,
If one day I'll live up as a dad,
If one day you'll say I love you to me,

Welcome to the world
Welcome to this place, Little One
Open up your eyes,
Look the world in the face, Little One,

I'd teach you everything over night,
That once you've found love to hold it tight,
I'd teach you to sing from a place deep inside,
That it's okay for a man to cry,

Welcome to the world,
Welcome to this place, Little One
Open up your eyes,
Look the world in the face, Little One. . . .

Written, performed, and recorded
by **George M. Dibble**, 2003

8

Tumbleweed - A Journey in Parenting

By Susan Bavaria

In autumn, the wind breaks the tumbleweed plant from its roots and blows it away. On the prairie with a strong wind, it might roll along for days, even miles. Each tumbleweed has a personality - round, oblong, scraggy, thick. It all depends on how long it's been tumbling around.

We watched her on videotape: a small, blond, waif picking at her shoe. She parked her gum on a tabletop and smiled into the camera.

"I live on a farm. There are two kids there." Her six-year-old voice made two syllable words out of "farm" and "there."

"Starla is my sister and Jamie is my foster sister. We have a dog named Moonbeam and new kittens." She smiles to the camera.

"If you guys . . . if . . . if . . . my new family lets me bring a baby cat, I'll bring Sylvester. He's the littlest one of all. I like baby cats. . ."

Words trailed off as her eyes wandered over blue carpet, brown plastic wastebasket, brown paneled walls - the backdrop for family visits during the last three years - the place where six dutiful foster parents brought whichever child they housed to see bio-mom and each other in weekly one-hour visits. Her dark eyes were alert and bright; she seemed happy for a kid in her seventh foster home looking for a permanent family.

"Do you know why we're making this tape?" asked the social worker.

"Because you want my new family to see what I'm like?" Half statement, half question. Suddenly a new thought lit up her face. "I hope I get my ears pierced for my adoption present." Pause. She hunched her shoulders, crinkled her nose and happily announced, "I'm done!" For a closing act, she picked up the gum, stuck it in her mouth, chewed it soft and blew a bubble.

We met with foster mom Nancy for a debriefing. Rose liked strawberry yogurt, Pintos and Cheese from Taco Bell, and plastic shoes called "jellies." She cut different size hearts out of old newspapers and saved them for her "new family." She yelled cuss words down the toilet and won the best student award in her kindergarten class. Her teacher, plus twenty-two other families, wanted to adopt her. Social Services chose us.

Double Black Diamond

George and I did not know then that we had chosen the double black diamond trail to parenting, the most difficult one reserved for experts or the foolhardy. At the time, it seemed an utterly suitable idea. We had married at 35 and 49, respectively. I had barely gotten my M.A. and was launching a new career as an editor. He had a daughter in college. The vague discussion of children before marriage was never very specific.

Me: "I might want to have kids, so don't rule out that option."

Him: "Okay."

Several years later found us not much further along the parenting continuum and enjoying the self-indulgence that's derigueur for the childless. I felt that if I didn't parent with George something would be missing from my life, but I knew he was content with the status quo.

"You know, I'm not sure I have the energy to have a baby," I said. "How about adoption?" "Let's look into it," he said. "Can we get one without diapers?"

Armed with a combined age of ninety-two and not a psychology course between us, we decided to adopt an older child. Only one county out of five in our area offered an eight-week class for prospective parents entitled *Adopting a Child with Special Needs*. We met in a library basement conference room for two hours every Monday evening. The teacher was an adoption social worker in her late fifties with curly gray hair, weary but cheerful. She was a mother of seven whose one Down syndrome child had died. She and her husband subsequently adopted another Down syndrome teen. By anyone's standards, they were heroic and selfless; so were others that we met. They laughed about tantrums, brushed off bedwetting. Undaunted, they reminded us of comic book heroes, batting away the challenges that assaulted them with a shrug and a grin. I wasn't sure that George and I were cut from the same resilient cloth. We were older, self-indulgent, and selfish with our time. We operated on the "no kids" default drive and were oblivious to the subtle way that a child encroached upon your life.

The class was enlightening - and scary. These kids harbored anger like a squirrel hoards nuts, dragging them out to gnaw on when the mood suited. Their stories stirred sympathy and wrath. Victimized beyond comprehension, their rage seemed understandable. These kids enmeshed their caretakers, peers, and everyone who entered their labyrinth of emotions in a draining cycle of manipulation and occasional dangerous acting out. Their parents, and most every other adult in their lives, betrayed them and some had shut down every avenue to a trusting relationship. You had to be a saint to volunteer for this duty. Were there any starter models for less seasoned parents, we wondered?

Meeting Rose

By the time we met Rose, we had served time in the foster parenting trenches and had the emotional hard bodies to show for it. We offered experience, education, and resources. Social Services awarded us the highest commendation - a child.

Rose was a fighter - a weed between two concrete slabs - an air plant without soil or roots. She and her three sisters survived through a meager existence of neglect, confusion, fear, and her mother's denial of sexual abuse by their father and Uncle. They ate a tedious diet of rice and peanut butter when welfare checks ran out and only landed in state custody when an aunt's conscience compelled her to report the abuse to authorities. On the brink of her fourth birthday, Rose was pried out of the only family she knew, moving through seven foster homes because of her feisty and demanding demeanor.

Turmoil and uncertainty had not broken her spirit, but anxiety forced her, at five-years-old, in her seventh and final foster placement, to drag a big cardboard box just outside her foster parents' bedroom. She slept in the box for the first week - a heartbreaking demonstration of a child on emotional life support, gasping for stability in a life spiraling out of control.

Experts say that loss and abandonment in early childhood can change a child's physiology - pain and stress shouldered onto neurological hardwiring that stays with a person forever. Some never recover from the trauma, and their lives are permanently on hold. Some react like a poked caterpillar - curling into a tight little ball and shutting down until the stimulus goes away. Some take anger out in passive ways, going into the bathroom and emptying all the shampoo bottles or stopping up toilets. Some spew their anger in a relentless barrage that wears you down, and that was Rose. Forty pounds of scrappy sinew, every cell geared for survival, she harangued sustenance out of a parched environment that withered too many others. "Loss is never completely resolved," said Dr. Vera Falberg in *A Child's Journey Through Placement*. "It may recycle in a variety of ways." Would it lie dormant in Rose like a seventeen-year locust to awake with a destructive vengeance at some unforeseen future date? That was the unknown variable, a crap shoot that adoptive parents face.

We met Rose at the farm one week after watching her on videotape. A pink vinyl photo album with a handwritten "Hi Rose!" peeking through the heart-shaped front cover preceded our arrival - the sum total of her new family in a dozen plastic sleeves. It contained magazine pictures - swimmers, golfers, a Boston iris - handwritten captions - Irises are my favorite flower, but now roses are too! - photos of our dog sleeping by the front door, 84-year-old Grandma Marge, George wearing a birthday hat with a "Mr. Clean" sign hung around his neck.

She and her sister whispered together as we drove up. She sported a new haircut like the Dutch Boy Paint logo, gave me a hug, and steered clear of George. There's a certain protocol upon meeting your new child that involves gift giving, and we decided on a book. I had gone to the best independent bookstore in town for help. ". . . For a six-year-old . . . our daughter. I don't know what she likes; we haven't met her yet. . ."

In her world, parents neither loved nor cared for children, so I didn't want anything sentimental. I settled on *Angelina and Alice* by Katherine Holabird from the series about two mice friends. A read-aloud story about two little mice girls with dresses and bows

who spat and found their way back to friendship by working on a gymnastics routine together. "Enjoy this book!" we inscribed, "Love, Mom and Dad."

Rose gave us a tour of her room, her perfectly-made top bunk because she never slept under covers. "I wrap up in Fred's blanket," she said proudly. The blanket was a handmade afghan she claimed like a grizzled prospector defending his last vein of gold. It was her most cherished possession, and her foster family gave it to her when she left along with the movie Annie. She barely let me wash it and always insisted that I save it first, out of all her other things, if we ever had a fire.

Gathering for coffee and cake in the dining room, we discussed a visitation schedule. Rose climbed on my lap, checking me out from top to bottom, the emotional equivalent of a white glove inspection. What did she make of olive metallic shoes and flowered socks? We discussed the afternoon visit, an overnight, and the ultimate nine-day stay which was the County Social Services transition plan for a child entering a new family.

A Beginning

"Now," I thought, "we're starting this right now." I felt overwhelmed. After years of thinking about and planning for a child, it was happening. Thoughts scrambled through my mind. How would she like my cooking? Would George's size-14 feet clomping down the hallway frighten her? I wanted this child, but I didn't love her yet. I began to mentally plan the purchase of her welcome home gifts.

Crisis struck the following week when Rose told her foster parents that George looked at her the same way that bio-dad-abuser did. She certainly forced this topic into the open to talk about what was her biggest fear. Would she be safe in our home?

Foster mom Nancy suggested that we read *A Very Touching Book* by Jane Hindman to open up the subject of what was appropriate behavior in our house. The book was clever and funny. Afterwards, George made a series of exaggerated expressions while Rose watched gravely to see if she could identify the look that scared her. He stretched his cheeks out in a wide grin, pulled his lips forward like a chimpanzee, popped out his eyeballs, raised his eyebrows up high then down low. She couldn't place it, but doubts about her safety never came up again.

I picked her up from foster care for the last time sixteen days after we met. Small and solemn, she stood in the doorway with clothes and stuffed animals packed in a big cardboard appliance box. Multiple foster homes and the burning of her family's rundown rental left only a few dresses from "Mommy" and two photograph albums. The one sister who lived with her had already left for New Mexico to meet her new family, so Rose was the last to leave the only stable home they had ever shared. It was probably tougher than she ever realized. She simply shut down and slept on the trip home. This gutsy little six-year-old - so tough and resilient - was being uprooted from

everything she knew to begin a new life with a family of total strangers - all before the start of first grade.

Postscripts: Since adopting Rose in 1992, we have traveled a singular journey as parents, at times lonely, at times exhilarating, always a challenge. Despite the most loving big bear hugs at night, family trips, skiing with friends or Compagnie Express clothes, you cannot alter the indelible stain of the past of an abused child. Puberty hit Rose especially hard with hormones, maturity, and history converging like cyanide dropped in a bucket of acid. "I have a tear and a flame inside of me," she said a year ago. "Sometimes I want to cry and sometimes I want to explode." She came home in April of this year to complete her sophomore year of high school after spending ten months in a residential treatment center for adolescents to deal with her deep-seated rage. We pray that her gifts continue to win out over her liabilities.

First published in the Green Journal. Susan Bavaria received a M.A. in Communication and Theatre from the University of Colorado in 1985. "Tumbleweed" is an excerpt from a creative non-fiction work-in-progress about her daughter entitled Cuddling the Cactus. *She works as a communications manager for the International Arabian Horse Association and lives in Denver, CO, with her husband George.*

"I can tell my friends

I never have to move."

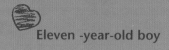

Eleven -year-old boy

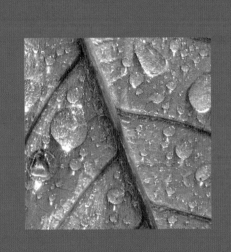

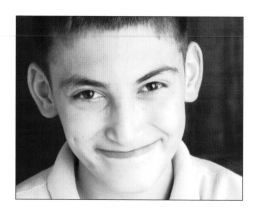

Dakota; Doyel Family; and Jasmine

Learning to Love

Attachment is a process, not an event. It takes time. For adoptive parents it begins with the decision to adopt and then going through the arduous steps of a home study, the search for the child, pre-placement meetings, and the placement process. Adoptive parents aren't perfect people, but generally their sense of esteem is strong enough to know they are loveable and have something worthwhile to give in a parent-child relationship. They make a commitment.

In *The Road Less Traveled* Dr. M. Scott Peck describes love as a decision, not an emotion. Mature adults make the commitment to love and allow the feelings to follow. They know that there will be times they don't feel a lot of "like" for a child, but they know and remember that they love their child.

Foster children have yet to learn the lessons of love. They feel conflict. They know they still love their birth parents, even though they've been told and witnessed that those parents are inadequate. They wonder if it is possible to love more than one mother or one dad and love them in different ways. Commitment is not a concept they grasp. Fear, memories of old disappointments and lack of self-esteem make it difficult for some children to bond with new families.

They enter the new family already traumatized by the past. The National Child Traumatic Stress Network reports traumatic stress can have a direct impact on the development of children's brains and bodies. Traumatic stress can interfere with children's ability to concentrate, learn, and perform in school. It can change how children view the world and their futures and can lead to future employment problems. It can take a tremendous toll on the entire family.

Attachment is important because it is the foundation for healthy adult relationships. It allows the child to mature over time so a commitment can be made to a job. The child learns to respect the boundaries of society and become a good steward of the community. Bonding with the new family allows a child to grow to believe he is loveable and enables him to love others. It is the cement which allows the child to form his own relationships and raise children of his own.

In normal infant development, the baby goes through a phase where it cries when its mother or primary caregiver is out of sight. The baby clings to his mother and refuses to be comforted or go to the arms of a well meaning friend. These months can be exhausting for a mom, who for that time is the sole source of security and love. That baby is attached.

Unattached children will hug anyone and some do hug almost everyone they meet. Adoptive parents long for the time when their hugs are special to their child. Sometimes it takes years.

Paul, an adoptive father in New Mexico, tells the story of asking the therapist "When will I know that my son loves me?" The therapist told him he would know. Weeks later Paul dropped his son at day care and repeated what he'd told him many times before as he said goodbye, "I love you." Patrick looked at him and said, "Duh-hh." That was the moment Paul knew. Patrick had grown enough to take his dad's love for granted! He knew he was loved. And he assumed Paul knew that he was loved in return.

Terry, another adoptive father, tells the story of waiting for his two sons to learn to love him. The attachment came more quickly for the younger boy, despite his brother's warnings. Through sound monitors Terry and his wife heard the big brother tell his little brother not to let himself like them, "We'll be leaving here too." But the children didn't leave. Terry and Paula continued to love their boys. And the night came when Terry knew - as he kissed his older son goodnight, he felt little arms reach out from under the covers to hug him. Terry's tears of joy blurred his vision. This moment was an important building block in their relationship. Parents can put up with a lot of adolescent testing, if they've had a few moments like those.

Elizabeth, an adoptive mother, talked to me about how long it took for her son to bond to the rest of the family. He preferred to sit in his bedroom alone rather than to engage with the rest of his family. "So were you patient? Did you give him lots of time to work that out?" I asked.

"Oh no!" She said, "I was in his face." He'd endured an adoption disruption and showed all of the signs of an unattached child, but Elizabeth begged to adopt him. She insisted he interact with the rest of the family, engaging him in all of the activities whether he wanted to join them or not. And ever so slowly it worked.

"When did you know you were part of this family?" I asked him. "The day I packed to go to college," he answered. He felt the tugs of sadness while loading his car and saying goodbye. He says he heaved a sigh as he saw his mom and siblings wave to him from the curb and said to himself, *I made it*!

In this chapter the Moran and Perley families, adoptive father Ted Roberts, teenager Shante Simpson and adoptive mother Diane Simpson, and Alice Weiss Doyle relate how the attachment and bonding stage impacted their lives.

El Viaje de Familia

First published in *Heartlines* Spring 2005

We are the Moran Family - myself, my wife Becky and our two adorable gifts from above - Patrick, age ten and Sarah, age seven. By birth, our children are 100% Hispanic. By way of adoption, they are 100% Irish. Oh, if they are confused now or in the future, as to what holiday - Cinco de Mayo or St. Patrick's Day to celebrate, who would blame them? There are about 114,000 children waiting for homes in the United States, and about 20,000 of them turn eighteen every year without having ever been part of a loving, caring forever family. With the help of The Adoption Exchange, that number will continue to be reduced, and it has been, by two already. We are here to tell you how this organization helped us obtain our "forever family."

What a long labor, but well worth it. Patrick and Sarah have been with us for about three years. Sarah joined us on April 18, 2002 and her biological brother, Patrick, joined us on May 8, 2002. For eighteen months or so, they were considered foster adopt children. We were followed by a social worker giving us advice on how to be good, loving, logical parents. Then on October 28, 2003 (two days after my birthday), after the mother's legal options in terms of appeal were exhausted, we finalized and they were cemented in our hearts after being born in our hearts a year and a half before. We continue to see a psychiatrist and a psychologist as well as any other "ists" we need to properly diagnose and help these two children. We have become their strongest voices, their biggest advocates.

They have made tremendous progress in our home but much more needs to occur. They would be considered children with special needs, as they are part of a sibling group, are children of color and have delays. Patrick is on a developmental disability waiver and will need services the rest of his life. Sarah has milder delays and, with time, hopefully, will be able to catch up. We have enrolled Patrick in gymnastics. He smiles from ear to ear when he goes and, after a year of trying, learned to do a cartwheel. He has done football, T-ball and earned a yellow belt in Tae Kwon Do. He has attended basketball camp and loves swimming. Sarah has been in ballet for three years and absolutely loves it. She is also doing tap and cheerleading. When Sarah first started ballet, she would not do it unless Becky was there doing it with her. Now, Becky can rest her ankles and knees as Sarah is doing it by herself. Sarah was afraid of the water when we first got her. Now, with the help of kickboards, she can go back and forth across the pool for hours on end.

Adoption is a hard, frustrating, emotionally gut-wrenching process, but one that is worth it a thousand fold for couples that have no other choices, like in our case, or couples that would like to add a "special" child to their family. One that they get to pick and choose. In our case, God closed shut and bolted a steel door but he opened a stained glass window of opportunity for us - for these children to be part of and share in our lives and call us "mommy" and "daddy." Ah, such sweet words and sounds.

The attachment process that children go through and the bonding that parents do has been very difficult, and believe me, there were times when we were ready to return them to the sender. But if you can withstand the holes in the walls, the pee all over your clean carpet, the pen on your walls and on your car upholstery, the whininess and the temper tantrums and defiance and sleepless nights, then there are rainbows at the end of stormy nights.

We had a lot of nights wondering if it was all worth it as we were holding them and comforting them in the middle of the night after a temper tantrum or bad dream, as they were calling us every name in the book. Believe me, they will keep testing you so that you will have to prove to them that you are safe and you are not going to discard them on the trash heap of society and move them to another house or get rid of them - as they have been accustomed to. They are good at pushing our buttons and they know us better than we know ourselves, in terms of what our triggers are. We used the love and logic approach of no emotion, no talk when they are in the midst of a temper tantrum, and then exuberance when they settle down and comply, even if it is two hours later. They are both developing a sense of humor. They both loved playing with dolls and stuffed animals and needing to be a baby. Slowly, they have grown out of that and have started to develop a strong attachment and knowledge that they are part of a "forever family." This is not a coincidence. There were too many spiritual connections in our journey - significant dates as evidence of divine intervention and my parents working from above to make sure it happened.

Now, as we close, we will answer the question as to which day we celebrate - Cinco de Pay or St. Patrick's Day. We celebrate each of them and the other 363 days as well with our new familia by way of adoption. A dream that came true because of kind folks like you. Hopefully, we can make the dream come alive for other couples as well. Thank you. It was well worth it. Having special children means having your heart live outside of you for the rest of your time. Being a parent means being sad when they are sad, being happy when they are happy, being frustrated when they are frustrated and being disappointed when they are disappointed but being able to wipe away the tears and tell them that they are a good, sweet kid.

- ♥ Being up in the middle of the night at the emergency room - $100 co-pay
- ♥ Tickets to an Isotopes game and seeing the wonder and awe in their eyes - $10
- ♥ Showing them how to fix something they destroyed - a cost of paint and nails
- ♥ Being adoptive parents and being able to hear the sweetest sound "mommy" and "daddy" - **priceless**

Thank you Adoption Exchange for making this forever family happy.

One New Family

By Ted Roberts
First published in *Heartlines* Fall 1998

A hot afternoon was brewing on the sixth floor of the Air Force Academy when I finally received the call I had been waiting for since I had finished all my parenting training. You know, the fourteen hour foster parent session, the ten hours laboring through potential problems your child might have, the hours of American Red Cross First Aid and CPR classes. The El Paso County (Colorado Springs) social worker wanted to know if I was interested in meeting an eight-year-old boy whom they considered a match for me.

Was I interested? I was darned well determined to get through with this and, oh yeah, I was a bit excited, too. I forgot to mention that I'm single - and I'm a male - both of which normally put you behind the person who is dead last in line. Fortunately, Colorado and particularly my county, recognizes the benefits to the child of having a permanent, stable home, and prospective single parents are just another resource. Single adoptive parents are not looking for special treatment. So just being "normal" is satisfying enough.

Mike is a tousle of blond hair, smart mouth, and pure energy. I wouldn't trade him for the world!

Reasonably representative of the kids who come into foster care, Mike brought with him some emotional and attachment issues. His birth father disappeared either shortly after Mike was conceived or born, I'm not sure which. Not that it matters, since he wasn't around when it mattered. His birth mother is an uncontrollable substance abuser, guilty mostly of neglect rather than physical abuse. She has been out of the picture for four years. Loaded with the emotional baggage of this uninspired beginning, Mike spent the next several years in relative and non-relative foster homes. He ended up smack dab on his own in Pueblo, Colorado at the tender age of eight, basically abandoned by a foster-adopt family unable to confront their own issues, not to mention those of a troubled child. When I received the call, Mike was living in a children's group home.

We met in June and he moved in on August 16, a little more than a week before his ninth birthday. The two months before he moved in were absolutely jammed packed with "getting to know you." Seriously, we talked for hours on end, knocking down barriers, building common experiences, and doing fun things. Yes, fun things! We goofy golfed; we visited the Royal Gorge; and we just started doing things together. Was it love at first sight - not hardly. Mike was a bit afraid of me and certainly didn't trust me to follow through on what had been promised to him. Why should he? No one had before. He certainly went through a process of doubt, reluctance, embarrassment, anger and resignation before he finally realized that I just might be the "real thing." For me, I figured since I was an adult who had wanted children for a long time that this kid was going to finally (and immediately) enter my heart. He didn't. Of course, I understood my responsibilities towards him, and I really liked him, but the gulf between like and love is, pardon the cliché, deep and wide. I'll bet it wasn't until Christmas time, fully six months after we had met, that I can truly say that I started loving him.

Mike is able to love unconditionally and completely, which is really an accomplishment considering what he has been through. He's a hugger. He gives compliments. He can't (won't) go to bed without being tucked in and about fifteen minutes of settle down talk. He does well in school and makes friends easily. The person Mike is today attests to his strength as a person and his ability to jump back from adversity. Strength and resilience, however, are only part of the solution. Hands-on parenting is certainly the most important factor in raising an adopted child. Yes, I said adopted, because on March 6, 1998, only six and a half months after he moved in, Mike's adoption was finalized in one of the speediest non-relative, single-parent adoptions in Colorado history. I attribute much of that success to three factors: demanding responsibility, ensuring consistency, and establishing structure. These factors are the very things that they harped on in all of those training sessions, and I, in my infinite wisdom (or boredom) kind of filed away in my "yeah, ok, so what" file. For Mike and I, they ensured success of our adoption. We are less than a month away from a complete year of living together.

From the days way back in 1995 when Dixie and her team came to Germany to spread the gospel of military adoptions to my not-so-accidental selection of Colorado Springs as my current place of residence, I have learned a tremendous amount about the adoption process, adoption agencies and social services, and most importantly about the children themselves. Mike and I have a loving relationship that is at least as tight as a birth relationship. I have been Dad from day one, and that was interesting back then. Now, almost a year later, we both know what "Dad" means and we are inseparable because of it.

The Adoption Exchange met Ted through its Global Connections program, a cooperative effort between The Adoption Exchange, Voice for International Development and Adoption and the National Military Family Association. The program expedites the adoption process for military families and U.S. citizens living abroad by providing them with easy access to information, resources, and placement services provided by qualified professionals around the globe.

You Know You Are in a Permanent Home if:

- You are introduced as "son" or "daughter."
- You have your own Christmas stocking.
- You have your picture on the wall. An 8 x 10!
- Your picture is on Grandma's wall.
- Your clothes are not labeled.
- You get braces on your teeth.
- You think of calling your social worker, and you don't have one!
- Your mom or dad sign your school permission slips.
- You do not worry about moving to another family.
- You go on family vacations.
- You stay with grandma, friends or relatives if your parents go on a trip.
- Your name is printed on family Christmas cards.
- You move with your family to another state.
- You stay with one of your parents if they get a divorce.
- You stay with the family even if mom or dad is seriously ill.
- Your parents arrange visits with your birth family.
- You know what school you will attend next year.
- You have a savings account, or a college fund.
- You can tell school friends about your next summer vacation plans.
- You are insured to drive the family car.
- You wear your mother's wedding dress at your own wedding.
- Your parents help you with a down payment on car, apartment, furniture, etc.
- Your mother becomes your children's grandmother.
- You can come home, even with your kids, if you need help.
- Your name is in the family will.
- You can inherit the family ranch.
- You feel that you "belong" in this family.
- Having the key to the house.
- Having someone to call in case of emergency (or when you have a flat tire on your way to work on your first day).

This is a light-hearted, yet pointed way of "testing" permanence. The suggestions for this paper came from adoptive parents, former foster parents and from former foster kids. Reproduced by permission from Costello Consulting, Inc., 2501 8th Avenue North, Great Falls, MT 59401

A Special Moment

By Shanté Simpson
First published in *Heartlines* Spring 1999

S hanté was born in November of 1981. With a
biological mother who was unable to parent
her, she found herself living in foster care and
shuffled between placements by the age of eight.
Shanté was registered with The Adoption Exchange in 1990
and we began to search for her adoptive family. What
follows is the remarkable speech she delivered to the
Adoption Exchange Association's National Conference in
October of 1998. Not only did she survive the instability
and trauma of many years of neglect, under her adoptive
mom's guidance and love, Shanté has matured into a
thoughtful, caring young adult.

"My name is Shanté Simpson and I am on the Junior
Advisory Board of The Adoption Exchange. My mother
is Diane Simpson and my grandmother is Irma Simpson.
I am sixteen and a half years old and a junior at
Colorado High School. I was adopted in 1991 when I
was nine years old. I met my mother at McGlone
Elementary School in Montbello, CO. I was in the third
grade and she was the social worker. Since I was in a
foster home, I had to see her to make sure my grades
were okay and that I was doing okay emotionally. My
brother was separated from my sister and me. My
sister was in middle school in Aurora. My sister and I were

taken to New Mexico to be on TV to see if anyone wanted to adopt us. We had two tapings out of state and then I did a taping here in Denver for an adoption party. I remember getting my face painted, getting balloons and having fun. They filmed it and it was shown on Wednesday for *Wednesday's Child*. I was on *Wednesday's Child* about four times.

About a year later, I was taken to a new home. That home was the lady that was the social worker at my school - my new mom. I had been told earlier that someone I knew wanted to adopt me so during the summer while the papers were getting finalized, I went to stay with her at her house. I was there for a family reunion weekend so I got to meet some of my new family. That was a fun day - the most fun that I have had for awhile.

On August 28, 1991, we went down to the courtroom and everything was finalized. I was finally in a home to call my own. That's where I stand now - in a blessed family and with friends. I thank God for the blessing of the life I live now. My sister was never adopted and is now struggling with a life of fear. My prayer before I graduate from college is that my sister is successful. It's because of me that my sister is alive today and has started college to become a nurse. I am very grateful. When I finish high school, I plan on going to a private Christian college to become an accountant. I may get my master's in Mathematics. I am on a Youth Power Team for the mayor. We have a team that does

community projects for kids my age. I have been in a choir called Voices of Faith for four years. We performed with Sinbad when he sang at the Paramount Theatre in 1996. In January of 1999, my choir is going to Tanzania, Africa, for a week and a half. I can't wait! The only thing I don't think will be fun are all the shots.

I enjoy my family. I am a blessed child and it shows in everything I do. If there is anything in life that a child needs, it is a family. I think no child should be lonely in these days. It only leads to destruction of a child's life. I hope you have enjoyed hearing about a short part of my life. I do want to thank The Adoption Exchange. I will always cherish this."

Since I presented this speech, I graduated from Colorado High School in January, 2000. I started college at Community College of Denver and then had a baby boy. His name is Keirryse and he is 5 years old. He is very loving and a joy to have. His smile is contagious and he's outgoing. I started to change my goals as time went on and began working for the airlines three years ago. I started doing customer service for two airlines and did this for three years. I am able to do a lot more traveling these days. I am starting a new position as a flight attendant for Mesa Airlines. I am excited about my new job and look forward to my son being able to travel, as well.

I have had more contact with my sister than my brother since I was adopted. My sister and I have kept in contact with each other through good and bad times. We have also helped each other out.

For me to be adopted was the best thing that could happen. I really have a testimony to tell and show the world. I am so blessed and thankful for my "walks" in life everyday. I enjoy my family and am a blessed woman. It shows in everything I do. If there is anything in life that a child needs, it is a family. I think no child is to be lonely in these days of so much uncertainty. It only leads to the destruction of a child's life. I hope you have enjoyed hearing about a short part of my life. I do want to thank The Adoption Exchange from the bottom of my heart for I will always cherish them.

As Shante's mother, Diane, I am grateful for The Adoption Exchange and its mission to match waiting children with new families. Shante' came into my life when I was seeing my life change from that of a young adult to a more "mature" adult. God brought us together and I am so thankful. Shante' and I have grown to become "women with a mission" to help others and be a blessing to others. I especially enjoy my little grandson and his enthusiasm for life. We have much support and a "village" that has become the wind beneath our wings.

Feeling Less Alone

By Peggy Perley
First published in *Heartlines* Fall 1999

In many ways, parenting our adopted children feels the same as parenting our birth children. There are numerous homework assignments, the sibling squabbles, the tattling, the appointments, and so on. But there are also differences.

With our birth children, the bonding came pretty much naturally, but with some of our adopted children, we have had to work at the bonding process very consciously. And we have had to learn a lot of new information about what attachment is and how it happens and what happens when a child can't form attachments easily.

Our daughter, who has attachment disorder, has learned some amazing ways to cope with the feelings she has from the trauma and disruptions she experienced. She learned to be combative with people. In our home, she has been defiant and refused to follow rules. For a time, it was very hard for all of us. We didn't understand what was going on. We just wanted to be a family, and it was so hard for her. We didn't know how to help.

I attended every training offered in my area of the state. I looked forward to every one. Listening to speakers and other parents made me feel "normal." I felt like I was in the same boat with all the other parents who have kids with these special needs. I came away feeling like our family isn't as unique as we sometimes feel.

An adoptive parent support group also helped me to feel less alone. It is a group of people who don't judge us when things are hard or if we have to be very strict when we have had to involve the police to help our daughter stick to rules. Many typical parents think we are over-reacting. In the support group, people understand.

Peggy Perley and her husband have four birth children and six adopted children.

My Greatest Heroes

By Alice Weiss Doyel
Written in memory of Hoyt W. Doyel

We all have moments in our lives that change us forever. Although we sense that these moments will be significant, it may be years until we realize why. It was in 1971 that I experienced two such important moments.

1971

When the first significant moment occurred I was twenty-seven-years-old. I met Little Mary. Her friends called her Little Mary because of her diminutive appearance. She had the underdeveloped look of an adult who had lacked nutrition and nurturing during her childhood.

Mary shared her experiences in foster homes with me. She had moved from foster home to foster home, sometimes doing house work, sometimes farm work, but always the dirty work. She had been mistreated, abused, and unloved.

Mary's manner of telling her story struck me even more than her words. When she spoke it was with an emptiness almost devoid of emotion. After hearing Mary tell her story, I knew that if I had a family it would include a child from the foster care system - a child needing a loving, forever family.

The second life-changing moment happened just two months later. Two close friends had me over to their apartment for a huge dinner one Saturday night. After dinner we went to a lively house party in their neighborhood. My friends introduced me to one of the party's hosts, Hoyt Doyel. The day after the party, Hoyt asked me out on our first date. By the second date we knew we were falling in love with each other. Before long we made plans to marry.

1981 - 1982

One decade later Hoyt and I experienced the true significance of those two life-changing moments in 1971. Two school-aged girls, Kim and Melanie, were adopted into our family. Our daughters became my greatest heroes. They taught us that we are all capable of defining our own destinies. Although both our genes and our past may shape us, we are still capable of directing and controlling our lives. We can determine our values and define our futures.

Nine-year-old Kim arrived from Methodist Home in Waco, Texas. Born in Seoul, South Korea, she moved to the United States with her biological family at age four. At age eight Kim was placed in Methodist Home, where she lived for one year before we adopted her.

Six and a half-year-old year old Melanie came to our family through Dallas Social Services. Melanie had been neglected and abused from infancy. The family's first referral to social services came when Melanie was one-year-old.

Multiple failures by the social service system harmed her significantly. Our family was Melanie's sixth placement during the two years she was in the foster care system. This included an adoption that disrupted. The social workers told us that our family was her last hope.

Becoming a Forever Family

Our new daughters, adopted one year apart, could not have been more different in both their genetic backgrounds and their experiences. However, there were distinct commonalities. Both of their lives were frozen in the past in many ways.

During her first years in our family, Melanie spent much of her time in a fantasy world. This was a world filled with fear, where she fought violently to protect herself and maintain control. Melanie saw me as her enemy and repelled my slightest touch.

Melanie's language was very limited and had its own strange syntax. I called it "Melanese". She had also created her own bizarre assumptions of the world that in no way meshed with reality. But sometimes I wondered if Melanie knew "great truths" about the world that the rest of us could not see. Melanie's metamorphosis began gradually. After several months we figured out that Melanie reacted adversely to milk. Five days after she stopped drinking milk, Melanie was able to walk hand-in-hand with me and even sit on my lap. Another important milestone occurred when Melanie played just like any child her age *for a whole ten minutes*. Those few minutes told us that anything, and everything, was possible!

Many adopted children emotionally return to a time and age when things were not so bad. However, Melanie had no memory of a secure or happy childhood. She needed to emotionally return to infancy in order to gradually move ahead with her life. Over the next two to three years she had to return to each developmental stage before emotionally reaching her chronological age, or at least something close to it.

While going back through these developmental stages, Melanie gradually let go of her violence. She allowed me to hold her and to rock her in my arms. Although it took many years, Melanie was able to put her anger toward "mothers" to rest. Melanie had finally figured out what it meant to be part of a family. She trusted and loved us.

Kim, on the other hand, had experienced love and care the first three years of her life. Within a few months of adopting her, Kim understood that she was part of the Doyel family. However, it still took her many years to achieve emotional security.

Kim had already experienced too many losses and too much pain. Bright and gregarious, Kim usually hid her problems and her fears. She kept them deep inside

her. This challenged Hoyt and me to be open and vulnerable in order to reach her. Our openness allowed her to gradually share her early life with us.

Hoyt even changed his personality, for the better I might say. He began to express his own feelings more openly and he communicated more often. He said if he didn't communicate well and express emotions openly, how would Kim ever learn?

Fortunately, communication takes many forms. Kim was an artistic child. She used her talents in numerous ways to cope with her life and to express her feelings and emotions: drawing and painting, writing poems and short stories, and doing photography.

Like most adopted children, Kim's and Melanie's lives were frozen in the past until they were able to grieve. However, they needed to feel secure before they could grieve. They went through the grief cycle many times. Each time they went through this cycle, they gained an increased sense of security, then grieved about the past, and then took their next steps forward.

There were great differences in our daughters' manners of grieving. Kim repressed both her emotions and her anger. She put on a pleasant façade, making her a superficially comfortable child. However, this was clearly a façade, neither normal nor healthy.

On rare occasions Kim would say just a bit to us about her past. We would jump in and listen intently at these times, regardless of who else was around or what else was happening. Once this window of opportunity closed, it would be weeks, or even months, before she shared her past with us again.

Kim was also too fearful to express anger, particularly at me as her mother. My mother and I agreed that I certainly had plenty of personal experience arguing with my mother as a teen-ager. I should be able to teach my own daughter how to do the same thing. Although this was a difficult process for both Kim and me, over time Kim learned to become openly angry at me. This enabled her to express her sadness and her anger about her past, allowing her to grieve and to move forward.

Melanie, having been abused since infancy, initially expressed her emotions with violence. Her violent feelings were directed primarily toward her first mother and me. There was nothing covert here! It was definitely a behavior that needed significant modification.

Melanie very gradually learned to express her anger toward her first mother in clear but less destructive ways. Some were even amusing. One time Melanie and I put all kinds of cleaning chemicals together in a bucket. Did it stink! We used this concoction to destroy a pretend image of her first mother in much the same way as Judy Garland killed the Wicked Witch of the West.

The last time Melanie physically displayed open anger toward her biological mother, she used my computer graphics program. She created an image of a woman, and then she made six black dots. She moved these black dots over the woman's body . . . killing her with these imaginary bullets. She had used a computer to express her anger instead of violent actions. After that time, Melanie talked about her past rather than acting out.

When Kim and Melanie first joined our family, their lives were frozen in the past in so many ways. They were unable to move ahead in a positive manner. Moving forward in a positive manner requires hope . . . and hope was a really scary concept! They were far more comfortable recreating the situations that had lead to prior abuse and rejection.

Hoyt and I learned that no matter how tough a child acts, a newly-adopted child is *very fragile*. Adopted children are *alone* in our world! What their first family did to them, no matter how horrendous, was often the closest thing to love they had. Children who have known only abuse and neglect must give up the violence that they knew as love in order to accept love that is gentle and caring. It took Melanie many months to even begin to accept gentleness and caring as love.

It became clear to Hoyt and me that the attachment adopted children have to their adoptive families is not instantaneous. It cannot be forced. It does not happen magically. It is not even inevitable! Attachment between our daughters and ourselves took several years.

Although most of our children's attachment to our family occurred within the first four years, we learned that attachment can always increase. As a young adult and a mother, Melanie's strong love and attachment to her own children also increased her attachment to Hoyt and me.

2006

Twenty-five years have passed since we became a forever family. Kim and Melanie are now young adults whose lives have gone in the direction of their hearts.

For several years after college Kim worked for a series of advertising agencies. She decided to return to college to study photography. Last year she spent three months traveling through South Korea and Southeast Asia, taking thousands of photographic images. After her trip Kim made the decision to make her passion and talent for photography a central part of her life. She is now in the throes of creating a new career for herself in this field.

Melanie completed junior college with excellent grades despite having learning disabilities. While working in a store, she caught the eye of a young man who came into shop. They soon fell in love. Today, Melanie and her husband are the proud parents of two young boys. Their first gleeful, energetic son was born in 2001. A second healthy, happy son was born in 2005. These children are growing up in their own loving, forever family.

I am amazed at Kim's and Melanie's ability to create such positive lives when they started with so many overwhelming challenges. When I feel discouraged with my own life, they are my role models. They are my greatest heroes.

Changing Our Lives

By Ronald and Susan Jackson

In the Spring of 1983 I was cooking dinner and watching the news. One of the features on the news was a segment called "Wednesday's Child" which was about a child that needed a home. The story was about a four and a half year old boy named Jesse. I was so moved by the story that when Ron got home I told him we needed to watch the 10:00pm news so he could see the story I had seen. We watched and decided that we should call about Jesse.

The next day I called and was informed there would be a meeting to talk about Jesse and The Adoption Exchange. We went to the meeting and found out about the process and were given the paperwork to fill out. As we drove home we talked about the process and that there were thirty-five families interested. We weren't sure our chances were very good but decided we'd give it a try.

About a month later we were called and told that they had narrowed it down to two families and we were one of the two. We were so excited and looking forward to the social worker visit to check out our home and us.

After the interview, within about a week we were notified that we had been selected as the home for

Jesse. Meeting Jesse was one of the high-lights of our life. Several weeks later, Jesse moved into our house and made our house a home.

Jesse brought a whole new dimension to our lives. We learned to be more patient, kind, and understanding because of Jesse being in our lives. We also learned to enjoy life more by laughing and doing fun "kid" activities. One of the best parts was the hugs and kisses we shared with Jesse and being called, "Dad" and "Mom."

We so appreciate The Adoption Exchange for changing our lives and that of our child. Thank you!!

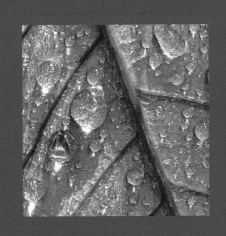

Keenan; Chesli, Courtney, and Rene; and Charles

The Honeymoon

His grandparents on the east coast had insisted upon adopting seven-year-old Michael when parental rights were terminated. Though his caseworker was skeptical, the placement was made. Two weeks later his caseworker and I were at the airport to meet this little boy who had crossed the country twice in less than a month. Separated from his brother, he'd been given a home with grandparents whom he didn't know, then had them taken away. He'd been rejected, put on a plane, and flown back to where the abuse and neglect had begun. He put on a courageous face even though he was alone again.

Michael's caseworker spent some time in a quiet place with him. She showed him an album of photographs of yet another new home and the family he would soon meet.

They had been called a few days before and agreed to adopt him even before they'd met. Michael wasn't interested in the photo album and I understood why. Anyone would be anxious and fearful in his circumstances. It meant nothing to him that this was to be his forever family.

A few hours later I drove away from the house of his new adoptive parents. I looked in the rear view mirror to see Michael running down the sidewalk in the opposite direction. After just three hours he was already running away, with his new dad in pursuit behind to catch him and bring him back home. Home? It wasn't home for Michael.

Remember the let down feeling when the big event is over? The guests are gone and the house is littered with party mess. Dirty dishes overflow the sink. Rooms that just hours before reverberated with laughter and good times are quiet. Furniture is out of place, strands of confetti hide on the floor, and empty glasses are strewn about. There is an empty feeling - a quiet loneliness that belies the earlier fun.

It is a feeling common to new families and adopted children. The euphoria and excitement of the placement wears off and daily living becomes an exercise. The honeymoon phase ends and the real work of putting the family together begins.

For adoptive families the honeymoon period can last for days, weeks, or months. It can even be years before the child's issues surface. For other families the hard part begins the minute the child enters their home.

The honeymoon period gives parents and children the chance to get acquainted. Parents celebrate their new family and children fight the fear they'll be moved again and try desperately to fit in. Nastassja remembers how she voluntarily cleaned house at every foster home "so they would like me."

Then disappointments creep in. Parents fear they do not love the child like they thought they would. There is a sense the child doesn't love them. The child's scars become painfully visible. Sometimes they are worse than their parents expected.

Parents wonder where their friends are when they need them. They are subjected to well-intended but off-the-mark advice like "just put the child in time-out." They suffer embarrassment and isolation when other parents don't want their child exposed to the new family member's behavior. They hurt when they hear "I told you so" and "You never know what you're going to get." They forget that life doesn't come with a guarantee for birth children or an adopted child.

Children struggle to find their place in this new unit. They marvel at the food, toys, and clothes. They try to adapt to a new school. Every routine is different. They want to believe in forever, but are still mired in the past. They dream about the future and have nightmares about the missing links of their lives.

Parents set goals and establish boundaries. They teach consequences for behavior. The child learns that home is a safe place to get angry, act out, make mistakes, and even do something awful. He won't be sent away. Slowly a new house becomes a real home.

One junior board member told me, "I will never clean another toilet." She recalled being required to do what she thought were the dirty jobs in every foster home. I wondered if she refused to clean the toilet in her adopted home and asked her if that was one of the early indicators that the honeymoon was over. She said, "Oh that's different. It's *my* house."

In this chapter Lani Tolman, retired Director and Trainer of the Family Attachment Institute; Adam, a fourteen-year-old adoptee; Shauna and adoptive parents Lee and Brenda, and adoptive mother Shirley talk about moving through the honeymoon into real life.

For the Love of Tony - A Mother's Story

First published in *Heartlines* August 1986

Whoosh….a soccer ball bounds across a grassy field. A herd of stampeding feet follows in hot pursuit. A small boy surges ahead, makes a sweeping kick, and smashes the ball into the opponent's zealously guarded goal. Elated over his accomplishment, a broad smile flashes across the boy's face. His attention quickly returns to the field, however, and the game at hand. It is still too soon to claim victory. In a sense the boy has already won; he has triumphed over an abusive past with the love and support of a new family.

The boy is Tony, a seven-year-old dynamo, bubbling with enthusiasm. On the sideline, his mother marvels over this courageous child who, only a year before, had never been a team player - had never been part of a real family. "Tony has come so very far," says Shirley Oquendo, Tony's new mother. "When he first came to live with us, Tony didn't know an A from a B, a saucer from a cup."

Born to a teenage mother, Tony was severely spanked as an infant for crying too much. Continued abuse and neglect alerted the social service agency which intervened to protect him. After attempts to work with Tony's birth mother failed, he was placed into foster care. By then, he perceived his tiny world as cold and hostile. Smacking a babysitter who told him what to do, or scuffling with a school chum who poked fun at him was not uncommon.

Tony shouldered other problems as well. He lagged behind in developmental skills and vented his frustrations through long, loud temper tantrums. Regarding him as a tough kid and a true survivor, Tony's social worker saw promise. Under his rough exterior, there was something very likeable about Tony.

Tony still had a lot of pent-up hostility when he came to live with Shirley and her eleven-year-old birth son Lawrence. Feelings of insecurity and worries over rejection clouded Tony's perceptions. "Tony was afraid that if he didn't act 'just right' we'd return him to foster care," confided Shirley. "Although Tony has made remarkable progress in every way, his most important achievement has been learning to trust."

An adopted child herself, Shirley and her brother were given love and new hope by parents who "really cared." That was one reason Shirley wanted to share her heart and home with another child. There were other motivating factors as well. "I always wanted to have lots of children," she explained. "But life doesn't always give you what you want. You can't stop living - or doing - because circumstances aren't just so."

Shirley decided that not being married wasn't going to stop her from having another child, so she turned to adoption. "It took about three years of work with social services to find Tony. He was worth the wait," she said. "Tony is just so great! The really neat thing about him is that he appreciates the little things.

When we're in a toy store and all the other kids are clamoring for transformers, Tony will see something ordinary, like a balloon, and his whole face lights up!"

Tony's innocence and love of "the little things" makes every event more rewarding. Adoption day was particularly memorable for Tony, his big brother Lawrence, and Shirley. "Tony had just graduated from kindergarten, so we had a double celebration," Shirley recalled. "The neighborhood kids came over, and we feasted on cake and ice cream; Tony was really excited."

Adopting a six-year-old doesn't come without trials. Shirley is the first to admit that there are still some bumpy spots on the road to happiness. "Tony is still learning how to control his aggressive behavior," she reports. "And Lawrence feels some sibling rivalry, but I think that's only natural. Luckily, Tony really looks up to Lawrence, and that helps."

Lawrence has proven to be a good role model for Tony. He has taught Tony how to work and play on the family computer, and Tony is jubilant over his new-found pastime. Speech and language therapy have greatly enhanced his vocabulary. Once labeled as having low-average intelligence, Tony is on target to enter the first grade.

"You just can't imagine the change in Tony over the past year," says Shirley. Perhaps all the joy and success is summed up best by Tony himself, as he takes Shirley by the hand, looks up at her with bright, shining eyes and says, "Oh Mommy, I love you!"

I Feel Safe

My name is Brian and I am fourteen-years-old. I don't remember my birth mother because she left me when I was about three-years-old. That's okay because I've heard that when she left me alone she tied me to a chair and put duct tape on my mouth. After that when I was living with my birth father he would leave me home alone. He physically beat me a lot. The trailer was never clean - it was always falling apart. My birth father got drunk a lot and I would be taken out of the trailer sometimes and then go back. When he tried to kill me with a gun, I was then put in a foster home. That was about five years ago.

For about four years I lived in a lot of foster homes. I would say that to move around a lot is not good. It got frustrating because I was always making friends and then I lose them, and start from scratch.

Almost a year and a half ago I was placed at a treatment center and was there for a year. There are a lot of staff for each kid and they pay a lot of attention to what we did or didn't do. There are a lot of rules. You wouldn't believe some of the things you had to ask for permission to do, like to get a drink of water. I learned a lot there, but it is a place I don't ever want to go back to.

After five years of being in foster care or residential care my birth father gave up his parental rights. The staff at residential felt I should leave there for a home again. I could have gone to another foster home but my caseworker felt I was ready to be adopted. I wanted to be in a normal, stable home, like I am now. I was video taped for a *Wednesday's Child* program. The people at the television station were really nice to me and …a little while later there was a big picnic at the park for kids looking to be adopted and adults looking for kids to adopt. My caseworker introduced me to Sarah and Daniel there, and we got to talk a little bit.

I was told that Sarah and Daniel had been chosen by the state as the family that might adopt me. We spent a day together and I felt right away they would be a good family for me. It wasn't only what they said, but how they acted. At residential they taught me to learn about what people are like from how they act. They like cats, and I like cats. They like to bicycle, and so do I. But I felt they were very nice people and that they would care about what happened to me. The next day Sarah's folks came in to visit and I could tell that they were nice people too and I liked the idea of staying with them and I told them so. First we spent days together, then overnights, and just before school started I moved in.

I've been living with Sarah and Daniel for less than three months, but it seems like longer. Now that I am in a stable home I feel safe and I am proud of myself because I'm doing well at school and in about three more months I will be adopted. They make me do my homework and get it in on time, but on the other hand, we try to have some fun. We go on walks and do family activities together.

Adopting is VERY important to me because of the life that I grew up in. I am not the only kid that should get adopted. There are LOTS of other kids that should be adopted too.

"Don't worry, Mom.

My sister will settle down after her adoption is finalized.

I did. It was over and done and I knew it was forever."

Shauna,
age twelve

A Wednesday's Child Is Now Home

First published in *Heartlines* Fall 2003

Angela was thirteen-years-old when Lee and Brenda received the call from the Utah Office of The Adoption Exchange informing them that there was a girl that would be perfect for their family. The first time that they saw Angela, she was eating lunch at the mall with her caseworker and was unaware that they were casually walking by. The next week, Angela's caseworker let her know that they wanted to make her a part of their family. After talking about it, she decided that she would like to live with them. The transition began with "dates" and "sleep-overs"; gradually making her comfortable with her new family. After six weeks, she moved into her new home.

Lee and Brenda have been married for fourteen years, and have two grown children. When asked why they wanted to adopt a thirteen-year-old girl, Brenda replied, "This is the one that God sent me. I prayed for her." Brenda and Angela have become very close and refer to each other as "good buds." Angela also gets along great with Lee. The transition, although quite smooth, has had some struggles and was a big adjustment for everyone. But the family spends a lot of time together and Angela is able to enjoy all of the things that girls her age should be able to experience. Angela has made tremendous progress and is doing well in school. She works very hard at everything that she does and is self-motivated. She opened her own savings account for college and puts money aside for her future. One of the special things that Angela has been able to do is decorate her own room. She has never had her own room before and it was a wonderful experience for her to be able to pick her own colors, carpet, and furniture. She has taken her first airplane ride to California and enjoyed a family vacation to Magic Mountain, Sea World, and Tijuana.

When asked what tools were effective in her family that she could share with other adoptive families, Brenda said, "Back off and don't expect too much at first. Never say negative things about the biological family. Try to listen and understand when she tells me things about her past. Don't say, "I understand or I know." I don't. I can only empathize. When she has to face tough memories or new information, I tell her how I would feel so she knows it's okay to feel that way. I just try to let her know that her emotions are all ok. And on a daily basis let her know she is loved."

"What helped us through rough spots? We read some book about discipline and how to manage our teen. We backed off when it wasn't important and continued to stress what we thought was important. For instance, a clean bedroom is not important, doing well in school is. We talked to friends who have teens to try to filter out what was normal teen behavior and what may have been a struggle to her because of her situation. Mostly, Lee and I talked in private and tried to sort things out. We talked about strategies to help her succeed, we united in our discipline plan, everything we did we tried to make it positive for her."

Parenting Our Wounded Children

By Lani Tolman
First published in *Heartlines* Fall 1999

It sounds like it should be easy. We're good and loving people. We give our children a lot of attention and tender loving care. We make sure they have what they need to keep them safe. Before we are into the experience of parenting a child wounded by experiences within their birth family and/or living in the foster care system, we tell ourselves that psychological and emotional wounds can't be *that* hard to heal.

How many times have we said those words? Well, it *is* hard! Very hard. Their wounds don't show. They look normal and healthy. It is, however, their behavior and responses to their hidden wounds that drive us over the edge. Most of what we learned in parenting classes, from our parents and from our non-wounded children does not work with our children who are severely psychologically and emotionally wounded. It is necessary that our hopes, dreams and expectations be compromised and redirected.

Getting down to the basics, we hope that our children will be able to have reciprocal and rewarding relationships; that they will be able to secure employment and develop the ability to support themselves and their potential families; that they will accept responsibility that is theirs; that they will not cause others pain and suffering, and that they will be able to experience feelings of well-being.

Our wounded children bring out the scared, angry, despairing parts of us as parents. We find ourselves treating them and feeling about them in ways that are unlike what we had ever envisioned. Some of the tips I used when I was in the throes of child-rearing were:

1. Make sure to have a good support group to call upon - people who understand and can support you as well as people who commiserate with you.

2. Find ways to fill your own cup. Do things that bring you joy and fulfillment. Make sure that, as a couple, you and your partner are on the same page.

3. Search out therapists who understand your child, as well as you as parents. It is not helpful if you are told that your child's behavior is due to your method of parenting.

4. Have a date once a week. Take overnights away with your spouse. If you are single, improvise.

Knowing childhood development will help you determine where your child is functioning. He may be on many different levels simultaneously. Look at the levels of emotional and psychological development and try meeting the child at those levels.

Lani Tolman has been involved with numerous agencies as a consultant and is recognized internationally as an expert in attachment, having trained hundreds of professionals and parents throughout the world. As a therapist and an adoptive parent, Ms. Tolman has personal experience to share.

"Adoption is a special kind of love

that is shared not by people who are related by blood,

but by people who are related by love."

Seventh grade girl

Heathcote Children; Devon; and Zahabre

Finding Themselves

Adoption is an uneven and sometimes inelegant process for children. In their roller coaster of life, highs and lows are magnified. As they move toward maturity, aspects of the past resurface to make these children question who they are and where they belong. Emptiness exists where love should reside. Teen angst is expressed through anger, outbursts, and turmoil. Fear of more loss forces these kids to harden their hearts or hide them away.

In foster care children lose contact with the people who make life decisions for them. Their many moves mean they lose a sense of their own history and with it parts of their identity. There has been no one consistent person to keep the stories of their lives intact. Looking back one man said he was so angry when he was little that he had difficulty liking adults even when they liked him.

The child wonders, "*What is wrong with me? If my family isn't any good, I must not be any good either. If I tell you what has happened in my life, will you believe me? Will you still like me? If I let myself love you, do I have to stop loving my first mother and dad?*" His sense of self is diluted or measured in ways that are hard for those who have not been through it to understand.

In their book *Beneath the Mask: Understanding Adopted Teens* authors Debbie Riley and John Meeks explain, "No matter what their adoption experience was, there appeared to be some commonalities among all adolescents. They all ponder why they were 'given up' for adoption; they have deep-seated thoughts and feelings about their birth parents, whether they had a prior relationship or not; and at some point in time, even for fleeting minutes, they have all wondered what they did to cause the relinquishments and were conflicted as to how to talk about this with their parents."

The authors go on to say that adoption is not the problem. "Rather it is those inherent variables in adoption that become the underpinnings of the profound complexities of the adoption experience during adolescence."

Dr. Joyce Pavao concludes there are normative crises in adoption. "A few of those normative crises are the extraordinary struggle to understand identity, often including, racial, ethnic, cultural and class identity; the feeling of belonging but not belonging; and the issue of abandonment."

Adoptive parents help ground children in life. The two most important gifts the parents give are unconditional love and an opportunity for the youths to begin to believe in themselves. Slowly over time, with someone to listen to them, the children begin to reshape their old beliefs. This has to happen before they can love.

That's why adoptive parents often find that they make the attachment long before their children.

Self-esteem is the value a person places on himself. Self-confidence and self-respect are the two important internal barometers that define self-esteem. Children need to feel competent to negotiate life and they need to feel worthy of living. A strong sense of self-esteem doesn't translate into perfection in choices or achievements or relationships or bodies. Rather, it is the notion that a person is equipped with all the tools necessary to make the best decisions possible with the information that is available at the moment.

Adoptive mother Jessie relates that through therapy her adoptive daughter Rachel learned that everyone in the family knew about her past and still wanted her, although when it came time to finalize the adoption Rachel became ambivalent. She liked her new family, but was afraid of making a permanent commitment. After a few trying days Rachel settled back into her new family. A loving home helped turn Rachel's life around.

Children who are loved begin to see themselves as loveable. They begin to believe they can contribute to the world around them. The basis for growth is in the messages their parents give them that they are loveable and competent. The foundation grows into a sense of integrity regarding how they live their lives.

Caseworkers and counselors work to help abused and neglected children let go of old, negative beliefs and discover their self-worth. The Education Center of The Adoption Exchange teachers caseworkers and foster parents how to help children create their own life books. These books are one way children can document their experiences, validate their losses, and piece together their history. As they put together the list of places they've lived and the people they've encountered along the way in a therapeutic environment, they can grieve and dare to understand that the behavior of the adults they trusted wasn't *their* fault.

Children have to be loved in life in order to grow up to be emotionally healthy. It can't be expected that they will grow up to respect others in their communities if no one has made a commitment to them. How can they learn to make a commitment to a boss, a mate, to their own children when they are grown?

Being emotionally healthy requires love of self and love of others. After these children have experienced unconditional love, they too can love. It's a life long process of healing, re-learning, and discovery.
In this chapter Paul, Sue and Dave, Jane and Fred, and Jessie talk about how their children blossomed in their loving homes.

Happy Landings

Written for United Airlines Magazine

Sonya is finally home where the pride and love that her adoptive family feels for her will nourish her spirit and make her strong. Jane and Fred, and their three grown daughters, have a very special feeling about Sonya. "The day we met her she was our kid. It felt like she had always been a part of our family but had just lived someplace else for eight years."

"We first saw her picture in The Adoption Exchange's photobook in the summer of 1987 and by October our little girl had come home!" says Jane, her voice full of pride and pleasure. "To adopt an Indian child was like coming home for me and I've loved the excuse to explore the old stories and Native American culture with her."

Jane's Native American heritage had been denied by most of her family, so having Sonya is finally allowing all of them to acknowledge and celebrate their ancestry. When Sonya first joined her new family, she also tried to deny her Indian heritage and would tell people she was Chinese or Korean. Now her favorite time of the day is when she nestles up against her mom to listen to stories about being Indian.

Adopting an eight-year-old girl isn't all smooth sailing even when you know your new child truly belongs with you. Sonya's seizures and speech and language delays have required a lot of attention. Helping her grieve the loss of the foster family she loved has also taken a lot of energy, love, and patience. But the struggles have been worth the effort. Sonya is doing very well in special education classes even though she had to change schools, which was pretty scary for a little girl who had already moved half way across the country to a new family. Her classmates saluted her for making the Honor Roll all year!

Because she was used to a large family and relied on brothers and sisters for playmates, Sonya begged Fred and Jane for "more kids." Three wishes were also granted in good fairy tales and last August Sonya got three sisters! The girls can usually be found happily swimming, turning cartwheels, or doing splits.

Jane and Fred's adoption experiences have left them with some strong feelings about foster care. "Sonya was our first adopted child and she spoiled us! She had an excellent foster home before us, whom we've kept in touch with, and her adjustment was so much less of a trauma than our subsequent kids had. Because with Sonya we saw how important good foster parenting can be, we are committed to keeping a place open in our family for at least one foster child at all times."

Is Sonya's family complete? Jane replied, "Not yet! We want one more and we know exactly what kind of child we are looking for! We want a child who looks more like our Princess (and like me). Everyone else is blond - like Daddy!"

The Adoption Exchange is pleased to be able to share Jane and Fred's appreciation for all who helped make it possible for Sonya to be finally home. Jane's words say it best. "Thanks for giving us our Princess!"

In 1992, United Airlines provided transportation to make this adoption possible.

A Loving Home Provides Traditional Values

First published in *Heartlines* October 1990

Baking cookies, writing letters to Santa, and participating in other family traditions helped thirteen-year-old Rachel adjust to her adoption by the Henderson family of Oklahoma.

When Rachel came to live with Jessie and her three children in March 1989, she had low self-esteem. "I did things to make her feel good about herself," Jessie recalled. "We went shopping for clothes and Rachel had her hair styled. It really made a difference because she loves how she looks now."

"Introducing Rachel to our values and traditions, like celebrating the holidays and attending family gatherings, made her feel secure and a part of the family," Jessie explained.

Jessie saw Rachel's picture in The Adoption Exchange photobook several years ago, but was told she wasn't available for adoption at that time. Later, when Jessie learned Rachel was still waiting, she drove over to the agency to get more information. Although there was some concern about whether Rachel would make it in a family after so many years of abuse and neglect and moving from foster home to foster home, Jessie's perseverance paid off. The adoption was finalized a few months later.

When Rachel moved in last March, Jessie, an elementary math teacher, enrolled her in the school where she taught. "She needed that closeness and one-on-one attention in order to bond. We were together on the way to school and sometimes we would make special stops on the way home, just the two of us."

At first Jessie's other children, Lawrence, sixteen, Gregory, fifteen, and JoAnne, fourteen, were apprehensive about Rachel coming to live with them. Jessie said, "The other kids were standoffish with her at first. Rachel wanted to be the only child and she called everyone dumb." To help the kids adjust, Jessie lined up an excellent family therapist. The kids are a lot more secure now, she explained, especially Rachel. Through therapy, Rachel learned that everyone in the family knew about her past and still wanted her.

Jessie has noticed lots of changes in Rachel over the eighteen months. "She has done a little acting out, but a lot less than she had been doing in foster care," explained Jessie, adding, "Her social skills have improved and she has learned not only to care about herself, but about others as well." Rachel has had a positive influence on her new younger brother and sister. Jessie hopes to adopt the ten and eight-year-old children soon.

As expected, good study habits are important at the Henderson home. "All the kids do their homework at the kitchen table," Jessie explained. "But Rachel couldn't do hers there, so I would have to isolate her. But the other night, I noticed her sitting at the table with the other kids, and I didn't say anything. Rachel and her sister, who are in the same grade, were studying their Spanish together. She's come a long way!" Jessie is especially proud of the fact that Rachel's grades have improved.

Although Rachel liked her new family, she became ambivalent when it came time to finalize the adoption. Rachel was afraid of making a permanent commitment. But Jessie was patient and told Rachel, "I just want you to do what you want to do." After a few trying days, Rachel settled back into her new family.

Jessie loves being a mom. The love and pride she shares with her children is obvious. And because of her love for her children, Jessie has helped Rachel develop a positive self-esteem. Finding a loving home has helped turn Rachel's life around.

"Getting adopted

is like sitting down

after standing up for a long time."

 Former foster child

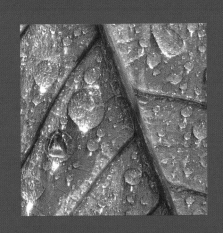

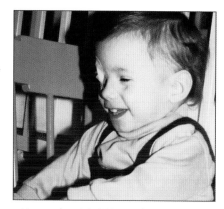

Jimmy Kennedy with kids and in action; Kehl Famliy; and Wayne then and now

Reaching High

When a child's mind is crowded with fear and loneliness, it's pretty difficult to imagine the future. When schools change, homes change and there is no routine, it is hard for a child to set goals. With no one to feed dreams it's hard to taste life's possibilities. Without encouragement and support it's hard to get past the fear of failure.

Nothing is more enticing than a beautifully wrapped package. The package itself is part of the gift. Someone has taken time to select the paper and fuss with a bow. The gift giver has taken care not to rip the wrapping or bend the corners of the box and thought about the colors chosen. And when the recipient feasts her eyes, a feeling of anticipation follows. Eventually, the package is unwrapped to reveal the treasure inside.

At The Adoption Exchange we think of the children as gifts we give the future. These precious packages have been jostled about, crushed, and bruised. They have been damaged and misused. The sharp edges of their contents have been left unprotected. Some are held precariously together. We hope the contents don't spill out and break before they can be safely delivered to the arms of the parents who wait to receive them.

Despite the packaging, we share with one another the excitement of discovering recipients for these gifts. We look for individuals who won't be put off by the size of the package or the smell of contents left untended or by the effort required to piece together broken parts. We look for - and we repeatedly find - people with curiosity, patience, generous spirits, ample reserves of energy, tenacity, and faith who carefully uncover the worn packaging and discover the treasures to be found. These are people who live with the stares and discomfort of strangers who don't understand. They are people who know how to celebrate the children -- their own gifts.

In his book *The Seven Habits of Highly Effective People* author Stephen Covey talks about the habit of personal leadership. It is the ability to begin with the end in mind. This vision of the finish helps adoptive parents avoid distractions and focus on aims that will produce more productive and successful outcomes for the children they bring into their families. Parents who adopt this mindset identify recreational and educational resources to help their children become good citizens, learn to make good choices in life, and find activities that help the children determine who they are.

Angela talks about the initial struggles with her daughter Heather. Heather joined the family at age eleven and a half. Her educational status was a shock. She couldn't count, she didn't know the months of the year, and she couldn't tell time. By the end of sixth grade she'd made the honor roll. Angela attributes the improvement to consistency. She and her husband chose a course of action and stuck with it. Heather has to be given credit too. She wanted to have a better life and appreciated what her parents did for her.

Heather's situation is not unusual. Foster children often attend a variety of schools, and are faced with disruption when they leave to move to another foster home.

Barbara remembers that when Phil came to them he had no speech. At over the age of five he wasn't even potty trained. Barbara home schooled him. Through trial and error she helped him learn how to process information. Now he is in a regular school program. His intellect and body responded to her love and patience. He has a chance at life he didn't have before.

In this chapter, Barbara, Jimmy, Melody, the Kehl Family, and Sue talk about children finding their gifts and the importance of setting goals.

We All Need to Set Goals

By Melody Roe, MSW,
Vice President of the Education Center

The Education Center of The Adoption Exchange provides training and consultation for adoptive families, caseworkers, adoption administrators, and therapists. Through its partnership with The Collaboration to AdoptUsKids (a service of The Children's Bureau) it works with agencies to establish their goals for policy and practice to ensure permanent families for children in the foster care system. For twelve months, a team representing the states of Colorado, Montana, Wyoming, and Utah met regularly to learn to "plan, study, and act" in ways that would result in changes to move more of the youth in care to permanent, lifelong connections.

The team included state or county staff, foster or adoptive parents, and teenagers from the service system.

At the last meeting in this series the young people on the team told the others that this initiative had been the most permanent aspect of their lives over the year. They knew when they would be meeting or talking by phone, knew who would be present, and knew that the other team members cared about what was happening to them. Others on the team were moved to think that this initiative was the most stability in the lives of these young people. How could it be! How could they *let* it be?

One judge commented several years ago that becoming an adoptive family is a two-way thing. The child has to adopt his parents, just as the parents adopt the child. By the time a foster child becomes a teenager, he sometimes wonders if he can trust any adult and isn't always sure he wants to allow himself to be loved - to be adopted. As the permanence team neared the end of its year-long initiative a faculty member and his daughter (adopted at age thirty-seven) spoke about their adoption experience. It was this presentation that helped one of the youth members of the team finally realize that she wasn't too old to be adopted, even though she was about to turn eighteen. She finally verbalized her discovery when she said, "I want to be adopted." It happened that her caseworker was in the room and took her message back to discuss it with her foster parents. They agreed to adopt her.

Another teen on the team stated that up to that point she'd never spoken up when she'd gone with her caseworker to court. In her state, youth are required to appear in court so that they are part of the planning for their futures, but she'd never said a word as she didn't believe she'd be heard. With encouragement from the team, she began to speak up in court and reported that her case has begun to take a new direction - the direction she'd hoped.

The team secured dental care for one of the youth, who'd spent months trying to get an appointment through one of the low-cost clinics. It became apparent that she had a couple of cavities that needed dental work when team members noticed she wasn't eating dessert at the meetings. She'd been told to call back monthly until an appointment would become open for her. That wasn't good enough, so team members stepped in.

One member of the team was put on restriction at the Job Corps and was told that he couldn't attend the final meeting of the team because he wasn't allowed to do anything "fun" as his punishment. A team member called the facility and reminded them that the meetings might be fun, but they were a commitment, too. This teen had been part of the team from the beginning and needed to be present for its last meeting where he could say goodbye and wrap up the experience. He was given permission to attend.

Parents give their children the things that these young people received from the permanence team last year. Parents give them consistency, stability, a chance to speak out about their own futures, acceptance, and even dental care. Once children are allowed to touch our hearts, the door to our own transformation is opened. There is no way that the adult members of that year-long team returned to business as usual in their service agencies. Their own goals of permanence for the children in the child welfare system took on a sense of urgency.

My Child Has Grown So Much!

Compiled by Jillian Hochstetler

According to a 2005 study sixty-five percent of children experienced seven or more placements while in foster care. The report was titled *Improving Family Foster Care: Findings from the Northwest Foster Care Alumni Study* and included 659 foster care alumni. The study reported that the rate of Post Traumatic Stress Disorder among young adults (ages twenty through thirty-three) who spent time in foster care is twice as high as in American war veterans.

The same year the University of Chicago identified four major education issues for foster children. They attend lower-performing schools. There are delays in getting them registered and starting school on time.

There is a high rate of school mobility - changing schools. There is poor communication among school staff and social services caseworkers regarding the needs of the children.

These factors probably contribute to the fact that adoptive parents consistently report that diagnoses of physical and emotional problems at the time of adoptive placement are inaccurate. There is power in stability. There is hope when the adults in a child's life learn to know them really well, when parents begin to set goals for their children and when the focus is on their abilities rather than their limitations.

We met one such family in Landstuhl, Germany, when we spoke at an adoption support group for military families. Angela wrote these words a year after Heather joined their family:

> Heather's educational status was quite a shock to us. At age eleven and a half she couldn't count except on her fingers, she didn't know the months of the year, and she couldn't tell time. She came to us in the fifth grade. The subsequent eighteen months were the most difficult of our lives as we struggled to control her behavior, temper outbursts, lies, manipulations, well, you know the rest!
> My husband and I can attribute the success we've had so far to *consistency*. We selected a course, and stayed with it! We've taught Heather that we mean what we say, that her actions have consequences, that she is accountable for her behavior, and her words.
>
> By the end of the sixth grade, she'd made the honor roll! During seventh grade, she's been able to maintain a high grade point although her behavior has not improved as much as we'd like. She loves attention and will do just about anything in class to get it. Her present school is quite strict so she gets detention, extra homework, etc. on a regular basis.

In 1998 (two years after Phillip joined Barbara's family) a member of our staff received a letter from Barbara, who wanted us to know about Phillip's progress since his adoption. "I came across this diagnosis for Phillip the other day, and just hardly recognized this as the same little boy I adopted." She included a copy of a letter his pediatrician wrote at the time he was about to leave foster care.

"He has functional autism, aggressive behavior and is a challenge to feed," the short letter said. "Phillip will require for the long term: 1) very intensive custodial care; 2) monitoring of his nutrition; 3) vigorous social and language stimulation; 4) possible medication for aggressive behavior; and 5) educational programs tailored to his special needs."

Here is Barbara's letter.

Some time ago you called me about a little boy who was listed in The Adoption Exchange as Phillip A. He had been listed for some years without hardly any interest. I ended up adopting that little boy in May 1996. That's when he became a part of my family, anyway. His adoption was not technically final until April 1997. I thought that you might be interested in knowing how he was doing.

This summer he learned to ride a two-wheel bike without the training wheels. When he first arrived we were afraid to even let him walk down the stairs alone he was so tipsy. He jumps on the trampoline and can even turn a flip. Some of the other children his age can't even do that. He got roller blades for his birthday and just put them on and rode off. Even last summer, he was fearful of trying new things. At this point, he is as big a daredevil as the other three eight-year-olds that we have. There is absolutely no evidence of an uneven gait. That has just improved this year. We got him a bike for his birthday last year and he could not pedal with his right leg. It had no strength at all. So we encouraged him to ride it and ride it. We began going on family bike rides. His bike had training wheels on it. He was so tipsy we didn't think that he would be ready to take the training wheels off for years. One day in July, we all went down to a church parking lot to ride and Phil said he wanted to take the training wheels off. We smiled at each other and took them off, ready to catch him when he fell and fell and fell. He just simply rode off and that was the end of the training wheels. He told us to throw them away when we got home.

I believe that he will be reading by the end of this school year. I home school nine of my children. He knows all of his numbers and can count to and recognize numbers to 100. He knows all of his letters and can identify their sounds in words. Last school year when I would ask him, for instance, "does dog start with a g?" he could never figure out how to answer that question. One day when I asked a similar question, he didn't try to answer it, he simply told me what letter the word did start with. I then realized that I was simply asking the wrong question. I began rephrasing a lot of the questions and found out that he did know what was going on but simply was not able to process some of the questions. We worked through all that and now he can answer any question you ask him regardless of how you ask it.

My kids go to AWANA, a church program where they memorize Bible verses. Last year I do not believe he was able to memorize one verse. This year he is going to the AWANA Olympics. Each child has to memorize ten sections to be eligible to go. Phillip has memorized twenty-four sections which is a total of forty verses. This is in a group of children his own age.

He has no evidence of any speech impediment. He had no speech at all when he arrived. He was not even potty-trained. He has no irregular gait, his so-called aggressive behavior is non-existent, he is the biggest pig in the family, and he is in a regular school program. I am so pleased with his progress.

He has been a joy from the very day he arrived. There was never any fitting in, he was just part of the family from the word "go." He is loved by all the children because of his sweet, giving nature. I don't know what his long-term outlook is, but you can't really know what any child's future holds. I want to tell you "thank you" for calling me. Phillip is the eighth adopted child in this family. We have Hispanic children, African-American children, and Native-American children in our family.

If you ever come across another child or children who you feel simply need a chance like Phil did, would you please give us a call?

Someone to Stand By Them

By Gary and Nancy Kehl

When an older child is brought into a home for a possible adoption, the child is generally suspicious as to whether or not the parents are going to really like him and make a long-term commitment. This is because they have generally been moved a lot throughout their experience in foster care.

When Edwin came to us he had only been in two foster care homes, but had lived with his Dad until he was eight-years-old. He had never met his mother until she showed up when he was eight. His dad's family was all black. Then this white woman shows up one night and says she's Edwin's mom and she's there to get him. He was surprised of course.

His Mom had married and had two little girls. He was moved to an all white family with a white step-father, who obviously did not like him. He called Edwin the "N" word and would say Edwin smelled like the "N" word. The mother took him to school and told the teachers he was retarded and would need special help. This of course damaged what little self-esteem he had and led to a lack of trust in adults. Then a church social worker got involved and convinced his mother that his situation was not a good one, suggested foster care, and maybe adoption.

After several years of foster care and occasionally taking Edwin back, his mother agreed to put him up for adoption. Nancy Kehl saw his name in a book listing older children who needed a home while she taught adoption classes for LDS Social Services on how to handle older children. She felt strongly that he should come to their home and convinced her husband, Gary, to take Edwin.

When Edwin showed up a little earlier than planned on June 15, Nancy and Gary knew this was meant to be. Edwin did everything he could possibly do to be accepted into the family. He got up early to shovel the walks if it had snowed the night before. He'd even go shovel the neighbors' walks, so they'd like him and say good things about him to his parents.

After being with the Kehl's for several months, Edwin had a problem he thought would most certainly get him sent back to foster care. At the church where his dad was the leader of the congregation, a boy had been pestering him and poking him in the back. Edwin had enough and punched the instigator in the nose. The nose bleed shot all over everywhere. Edwin's bothers and sisters said, "Oh boy now you've done it you'll be on your way back."

After arriving home from church Nancy wanted to know where Edwin was. She found him hiding in the basement. She took him into his bedroom and said, "Son I understand you had a problem at church."

He just shook his head and said, "I guess."

Nancy put her arm around him and said, "Son did your Mom ever tell you she loved you?" He shook his head no. She asked, "Did your foster Moms ever tell you they loved you?" He shook his head no.

Then with her arms tightly around Edwin she said, "Son I want you to know that I love you and know no one is going take you away or send you away, this is your home." Edwin put his head on her shoulder and at age thirteen cried like a baby.

Edwin later told us that was the day he knew he was home, and that someone really did love and care for him.

Everyone in this life deserves to know that someone loves them and cares for them. If the adopted child makes a mistake, as we all do, they need to know they will have someone to stand by them and help them through.

Although he had never played organized sports before he was thirteen, Edwin went on to play football and became a star in high school. Then he started for four years at Brigham Young University as defensive end, graduated from BYU with a degree in psychology, and played football in the NFL and NFL Europe for four years before he retired. He now owns his own car dealership, America's Auto Group. He is married and has three children, one a full African-American little boy named Jaden, whom they adopted.

Hard Work: A Ticket Out

By Rob Rains, sportswriter and author of *Mark McGwire Home Run Hero* and the *St. Louis Cardinals' 100th Anniversary*

Jimmy Kennedy's troubled childhood included being separated from his mother and moving into and out of a foster home, a poor relationship with his father, and being assigned to special education classes because of his unruly behavior.

Kennedy was cut twice from the junior high football team in Yonkers, New York, but he suddenly hit a growth spurt between the eighth and ninth grade. In six months, he grew from a 5'6", 145-pounder into a 6'2", 255 pound future All-American. He later resumed living with his mother and two younger brothers. His mother had overcome some personal problems, but was still struggling financially to care for the family.

Jimmy needed money for clothes. He lived in a tough neighborhood. He was not doing well in school. He was suffering from low self-esteem and did not have a plan for his life. When he missed too many classes his freshman year, he was told he would have to repeat that grade.

It was during his second year as a freshman at Roosevelt High School that his life changed thanks to Tony DeMatteo, the school's football coach.

"I was selling drugs," Kennedy admitted. "My high school coach caught me making a drug sale at the school. I also had a gun on me. He told me that I had to try out for the football team starting the next day or he was going to press charges."

It was an easy choice to make. For the first time in his life Kennedy was about to succeed at something. DeMatteo impressed upon him the need to straighten out his life. The coach explained that football could be Kennedy's ticket out of the rough neighborhood and an uncertain future.

Because of his size, quickness, and athletic ability; it wasn't long until colleges began to notice Kennedy. He became more focused at school.

"I knew that if I did not get a scholarship I wasn't going to college," Kennedy said. "My coach also told me the statistics about how small a percent of high school football players get a scholarship and then how few of those players actually get to play in the NFL. I had to prepare myself for more than football."

After starring at Roosevelt for three years, Kennedy accepted a scholarship to Penn State, one of the leading football powerhouses in the country; but also one of the most challenging academic schools. He was ineligible to play football as a freshman, because of low test scores, and that again provided him motivation to work as hard in the classroom as he was on the football field.

"When I left to go to Penn State I didn't go back to New York until after I had my degree," Kennedy says. "I stayed up there every summer, going to school and working out. I knew if I did well enough in school football would take care of itself."

Kennedy earned his degree in rehabilitation services education in four years. He also became an All-American defensive tackle and a first round draft pick of the St. Louis Rams in the 2003 draft, the twelfth overall selection.

Because of his hard work and dedication, both in school and on the football field, he had made his dreams come true. He knows from personal experience that life isn't easy and he is more than willing to support organizations such as The Adoption Exchange because he knows he would not be where he is today without the help and support he received from others as he grew up.

He grew close to his parents again over the years and is trying to pass along some of his lessons learned to his own two sons, seven-year-old Dyani and ten-month-old Devan.

"I'm fortunate to have a car and a truck now, but I didn't own a car until I was almost out of college," Kennedy says. "Dyani doesn't know what a privilege it is to ride to school everyday. One day he insisted he should ride in the car and not the truck. So that day and for the next two weeks, we walked to school. I want to make sure he understands and appreciates what he has."

Celebrating His 25th Adoption Anniversary

By Jillian Hochstetler

Each year the Vaughan family celebrates the anniversary of Wayne's adoption. In 2007, however, they decided to go all out in celebrating Wayne's 25th Adoption Anniversary. Over one hundred forty people turned out for dinner and dancing in honor of Wayne's adoption and his life. Among the group were people who Wayne had touched throughout the years: his parents, his four siblings, grandparents, relatives from across the country, his pediatrician, his childhood baby sitter, friends, Love Sac employees, Wendy's employees, and staff from The Adoption Exchange.

In October of 1981, B. Wray Vaughan saw a tiny little boy named Wayne on a *Wednesday's Child* broadcast on KCNC News4. Wayne was two and a half years old and weighed only fourteen pounds. He not only had cystic fibrosis but was also considered "failure to thrive". His wife Kathy was sleeping and when she woke up the next morning B. Wray told her about the child that just got to him the night before. As they began to think seriously about adopting Wayne, they saw him in a *Denver Post* article about an Adoption Exchange adoption party, and again in an advertisement for an Adoption Exchange telethon.

"What? " her husband asked Kathy, "Do we need to be struck by lightening here?" They agreed that it was meant to be.

Now, twenty-five years later, there is much to celebrate. "It has been a real blessing to see Wayne accomplish so much," said Kathy. "We've learned that Wayne can accomplish anything he puts his mind to." Among Wayne's accomplishments over the past twenty-five years have been graduating from high school, achieving his dream of obtaining a driver's license, qualifying at the state level for the Special Olympics Ski team, and being named Employee of the Month at Wendy's. As Wayne said, "My sister Cassie told me 'you can do anything you decide to do.'" Advice Wayne has definitely taken to heart.

Wayne's best friend since preschool, Patrick Hopper, who is now an electrical engineer in Seattle, shared in the festivities. With arms draped affectionately across one another's shoulders, Patrick proposed a toast to Wayne. "Wayne has been my best friend since we met in the sand box when we were four years old. Any time I've needed him, he's been there for me. When you know Wayne, it's easy to forget what he has overcome to achieve all that he has. He was told he'd never read or write, but Wayne loves email. And — sorry mom and dad — he's a lot better on the computer than my parents! He was told he couldn't do it, but he got his driver's license. I have so much respect for him and what he has accomplished."

The Vaughan family hopes Wayne's story inspires others to adopt, and displayed at his adoption celebration photos of children still waiting for their forever family.

Then...and...Now

By Sue and Dave Heathcote
First published in *Heartlines* 1999

Twenty-four days after her fourth birthday, Sheree and her seven-year-old sister, Vivian, were placed in shelter care. Alone, adrift, and without anyone..they knew or loved, she and her older sister were suddenly "wards of the state" - dependent on the kindness of strangers and thrust into a life of uncertainty.

Despite trauma and five subsequent moves in care, both girls were described as "sweet, happy, lovable children." When they were finally listed with The Adoption Exchange in May 1997, these remarkable sisters had been able to survive and thrive due to their own emotional reserves and the support of nurturing foster parents. What they really needed was a permanent family to call HOME.

In the summer of 1997, while looking at the new listings of children awaiting families with The Adoption Exchange, we saw a set of two sisters for whom we thought we could be the best family. We phoned The Adoption Exchange and were connected with their social worker. Our local agency sent our home study and several weeks later, to our joy, we were told that we had been accepted as the new family for Vivian and Sheree, a sibling set of sisters, ages six and nine. Initially, we connected with the girls by sending them photo albums which showed our house, the yard, myself, my wife, and the brothers and sisters who would make up their new family. Labels were attached to each picture, including shots of their new school, classmates, and teachers. We were fortunate that our new daughters had spent the previous two years with excellent foster parents. A mature couple, whom the girls called Grandma and Grandpa, they had worked with love and patience to prepare our daughters to enter a new home with a new "mom and dad." Also essential for success was the willingness of these sisters as well as our existing children to accept other faces that would be looking for love and attention from their parents.

This is not the Brady Bunch. We have many of the same ups and downs as other families. The girls disagree about who is doing what chore, whine about bedtime, think that TV is more important than eating, and feel that Barbie's new outfit is infinitely more interesting than that late school assignment. Our youngest daughter requires special education services and is now in an excellent program. We are working very hard at teaching her to read. We had totally forgotten how wearing a seven-year-old can be with endless chatter, particularly when stuck in the "why" mode!

Our older "new" daughter needs a lot of help to organize her schoolwork as well as nudges to remember to do it. She also needed to learn that we do not expect perfection in our children, nor are we perfect parents. Everyone takes time to fully adjust to a new family or new family members. The bottom line is that our two new daughters have made steady progress since entering our home over a year ago.

They do miss people that they left behind and some elements of their life in Colorado. They keep in touch by phone with their foster parents and never hesitate to run to the phone if their caseworker calls. As with many children, five minutes on the phone is usually all that it takes to touch base, but that contact is vitally important to maintain.

We have been truly blessed to receive our wonderful new daughters, courtesy of God and The Adoption Exchange.

Like most parents, we wonder where the time has gone. The two diminutive sisters that arrived in 1997 are now grown young women. Vivien's high school graduation was last year (although she is still 2 courses short and working on them), and Sheree is now in grade 10. To everyone's great joy, their US foster parents (still referred to as Grandma and Grandpa) made the trip to Canada to attend Vivien's high school graduation ceremonies in May of 2006. Four of our 5 Americans spent two years with Grandma and Grandpa and they are greatly loved and needed in their life as they continue to grow. Hurray to foster parents!!!

Our family has grown since 1997, with the adoption of three more children from Denver. Brandi (now fifteen) arrived in 1999, and a brother and sister team, Devon (now fifteen) and Kiara (now 13) arrived in 2001. Two of these three last arrivals were having some severe behavioral problems immediately before placement. It has not been a smooth ride to say the least, but there has been steady improvement and rounding off of the sharp edges. All three attend school regularly without protest, and are trying their best to succeed. Three of the five have part-time jobs, the continuation of which depends on steady efforts in school.

All 5 are coping with the legacy of their bio parent's addiction to drugs, alcohol or both. Learning difficulties require special education programs and medications to achieve focus and attention span in school. Sheree is affected the most physically and cognitively and we deal with Juvenile rheumatoid arthritis and degenerative bone disease in her feet. Her ankles, knees and wrists frequently swell when over used, and she cannot participate in gym classes. Every month or so she is on crutches for several days until her the swelling goes down. Her arms are abnormally constructed, which makes hand work difficult. She has a very pleasant personality, and faithfully does everything the doctors tell her to do. She would like to have a part time job, but regular school attendance takes 100% of her effort. We have found an agency that works with disabled people to find suitable employment and plan to have Sheree go there after grade twelve. The agency has been successful with 3 of her older sisters.

Devon arrived with ODD, Conduct Disorder and FASD. The early years (2001) were not easy and defiance is still in existence. In 2007, Devon started part time as a dishwasher at a local restaurant. His efforts there were so noticeable that they are now training him as a cook. Brandi (1999) has been a difficult child also. It has taken years for her to bond and it is still a somewhat tenuous

bond. In spite of this, she is a really good kid who works hard in school and we love her dearly. Brandi has also worked in the food industry, first as a stock person in a grocery store, and now in an ice cream shop. They are motivated to learn the job routines to produce a paycheck. A secondary positive effect we have noticed is they are also training their minds to retain facts; procedures and organizational abilities that help get the school work done.

After adopting a total of ten older children equalling twelve altogether, we can tell you this. Given the chance to become productive members of society, our older adopted kids have all grabbed on to the opportunity. There is no question that they are bonded to this family, yet retain pride in their heritage and where possible, contact with bio-family members. The youngest was six and the oldest was twelve when they came to this family. Our oldest adoptees are now in their mid twenties. When your life is interrupted, there are delays. It takes them to about the age of twenty five to settle into their adult roles and be ready to take on the world on their own terms. The older ones are marrying, raising successful families and have blended into the community.

They are all becoming productive young adults and we are tremendously proud of them.

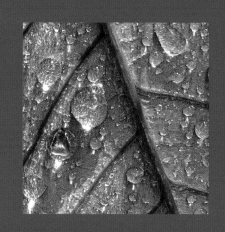

Justin, Jennifer, Heather and Stephanie; Zachery; and Alexis

Brothers and Sisters

At a recent adoption party at White Fence Farm two brothers arrived with their foster parents. They let the staff know their sister was expected to attend. She had been adopted a few months earlier and the boys were ecstatic when they caught sight of her. First they shouted, "There's Michelle," then they hugged. They looked at one another and then hugged again. Over and over Michelle touched the tops of her brothers' heads. "I am going to sit with Michelle," her brother, Dylan said. He grabbed her hand and they joined the buffet line for lunch, leaving several adults with eyes too misty to find their way in the dining room.

When separated, older children worry a great deal about their younger siblings. Often they have been the substitute parent. Linda, a sixteen-year-old, writes that she liked having a mom and dad for herself and her brothers and sisters so she didn't have to be the mom any more.

Conrad was six-years-old and didn't realize he had a half brother. When he entered foster care he was reunited with his big brother, Kenny. Though their birth mother loved them, she was unable to keep them safe because of her own disabilities. At age twelve Conrad was adopted by Buddy. Buddy, a career teacher of children of military families, lived in The Netherlands. Conrad grew up on military bases in Germany, Korea and Okinawa.

Buddy made sure the boys stayed in touch, though Kenny had refused adoption. Despite the miles between them Conrad said it felt more like he had a brother after he was adopted than when they lived in the same city. Video tapes, email, and phone calls kept their connection intact. Buddy brought the boys together for family vacations. On one trip to the states, they made a point to visit the boys' birth mom. That night Buddy told me how it broke his heart to see the virtual shrine she'd made from the pictures of Conrad that his adopted dad had sent her. But there were no pictures of Kenny. Buddy went home and sorted through photographs until he found some of Kenny that he could send.

Debby and Alan saw a *Wednesday's Child* on KCNC CBS4 that featured five beautiful children ages one to five who desperately needed a home. After discussion with their three older birth children, Debby and Alan made the decision to adopt. Blending the family into a unit of ten was not easy. The five adopted children had been separated and were living in different foster homes. The three oldest had not fully realized all the sacrifices they would make in lost time and attention from their mom and dad.

"After a honeymoon period, we had to deal with sibling rivalry. In a way it was like blending three families into one," Alan remembers.

Debby says the adoption has made them a better family. "We've become a close group and the kids are very protective of one another."

Melanie recalls a rough beginning when James joined their family. "James never had any preparation time and his behavior in school was awful. I thought I was prepared and could immediately love any child that came through the door. The children had an easier time than I did. They really stood by James and made him feel like part of the family." Today James has made a ninety percent turnaround at school and is winning ski medals in Special Olympics.

Suzanne spoke of the hurt inflicted by well-meaning people when they would ask which children were hers. "My response was always 'all of them.'" Her answer reaffirmed for her children that they are all equal in her heart.

Sherry thought hard about adding four children to her family knowing that six children under the age of seven in a house with one bathroom would be a challenge. Now the family thrives. Sherry says, "The children have learned to be more independent and have learned to help each other."

The ability to keep siblings together and to have birth children welcome adopted children as brother and sister positively impacts the sense of belonging so critical to children as they grow.

In this chapter Sherrie and Milne, Suzanne, Debby and Alan, Pat and Mike, and Ben and Melanie speak to the impact birth and adopted siblings have on families.

There are over 580,000 children in foster care

across the United States.

65% - 85% of children entering the foster care

system have at least one sibling.

30% of children in foster care have four siblings or more.

75% of siblings end up apart when they enter foster care.

THREE OUT OF FOUR CHILDREN PLACED IN FOSTER CARE

ARE SEPARATED FROM AT LEAST ONE SIBLING

A Warm Home in Alaska

The pitter-patter of tiny feet sounds more like a thundering stampede at the home of Milne and Sherry. A herd of smiling faces with deep shining eyes crowds the dinner table each night as the family gives thanks for their blessings - the greatest of which is each other.

Billy, Candace, Katie, and Tony ranged in age from one to five when they lived with their foster family in South Dakota. These beautiful Native American children now call Milne and Sherry "Dad and Mom" and call Alaska home.

First published in *Heartlines* February 1988

It was the family's social worker who first saw the children pictured in the pages of The Adoption Exchange's photobook. She immediately contacted a family living on an island reservation in Alaska. Milne and Sherry had already adopted two Sioux brothers and these three seemed to be a good match.

Sherry, a nurse, and Milne, who is a tribal judge on the reservation, decided to give this adoption strong consideration. Sherry and her mother flew to South Dakota to get acquainted with the children. Sherry fell in love and was particularly impressed with their energetic social worker.

"Deciding to actually adopt the kids, however, was the hardest thing we've ever done," admits Sherry. "Six children all under the age of seven in a house with one bathroom has been a challenge!"

Because giving names is an important tradition in Native American culture, Sherrie and Milne proudly bestowed new first or middle names upon their newly adopted children. They are now Billy, Bethany, Melody, Joy, and Christian. Erik and Mark, previously adopted from South Dakota are now Milne, Jr. and Mark.

Sherry and Milne report that becoming a family was a difficult process at first. "It's hard to understand the grieving process the children go through," says Sherry. "The girls were particularly attached to their foster parents in South Dakota. All the children get along beautifully, which has really helped. Milne and I kept saying we'd give the adoption another day. The days added up and things finally got better."

The children have learned to be more independent and have learned to help each other. Sherry has learned a lot too. She has learned to adjust to prevailing conditions. For example, she and Milne had planned to use cloth diapers initially, but found that to do so required them to rise at 3:00 a.m.! Thus, they quickly changed to disposable diapers.

Milne, who uses a wheelchair, says the children love him because he takes them to basketball games and showers them with hot dogs and soda pop. Despite the challenges of a wheelchair, there is much more to love in this gentle man. One of the children's favorite games is "wheelchair" where they push each other around the house in rocking chairs.

The family is thriving these days. They recently acquired a van especially equipped for Milne with enough seat belts for all eight. The family now hopes to add three bedrooms and, of course, another bathroom to their home.

"The best part of the adoption has been the knowledge that they are ours and we are theirs," says Sherry. "And they have a place to call 'home' - forever."

Benji Finally Has a Brother

First published in *Heartlines* October 1991

One fall day Ben and Melanie glanced out the window and saw their son, Benji, then eight, wandering around the driveway looking forlorn. Benji's two younger sisters, Amanda and Laurie, were off playing together. That's when they realized Benji needed a playmate of his own.

Ben and Melanie were willing to accept a child with disabilities and they wanted a boy for Benji, who has mild cerebral palsy and mental retardation.

Some time later the family attended an adoption party and saw James' picture in the photobook. They knew then that they'd found their little boy. "James was the only child we requested," Melanie said, adding, "And our request was his only offer for a permanent home, too." Although James, then eight-years-old, is legally blind and has some mental retardation, that didn't stop them from pursuing their goal.

The family traveled to Nevada for their first visit with James. At the time, Ben and Melanie told their children not to get their hopes up because "they are still working out the details and James might not be our child." But Benji knew differently. When they arrived and saw James playing with his trucks in the driveway of his foster home, Benji shouted, "There he is - the brother!"

Shortly before school started that summer, James came to Colorado to live. The next several months were a very difficult time for both him and the rest of the family. "I cried almost every day for seven weeks," Melanie said. "James never had any preparation time and his behavior in school was awful. I thought I was prepared and could immediately love any child that came through the door. The children had an easier time than I did. They really stood by James and made him feel like a part of the family."

By fall, James was calling his new parents "Mom and Dad" and his behavior was starting to change. Today James fits right in and the children argue like siblings do. Benji has even accepted more responsibility and acts like a big brother to James. But the most noticeable improvement has been in James himself. He is win-ning skiing medals in Special Olympics and the school psychologist told Ben and Melanie that James has made a ninety percent turnaround at school. Best of all, Benji has a brother.

Eight Is Enough

First published in *Heartlines* February 1990

Five years ago, Debby and Alan, along with their three children, would have shaken their heads in disbelief if told their family of five would expand to ten. The Denver area family's disbelief turned into a family goal after they saw *Wednesday's Child* in early 1988. The program featured five beautiful children who desperately needed a home. Their ages ranged from one to five.

We just couldn't get those kids out of our minds," Alan says. "Our goal was to see that the kids stayed together. We saw a need and knew we could fill it." The decision to adopt Jamie, Joshua, Michaeleen, Matthew, and Christopher was an easy one. When Debby and Alan discussed the idea with their birth children (Matt, Jenny and April), the decision was a resounding "yes." Three, just wasn't enough for this family.

The arrival of the children meant the family faced lots of adjustments. The first change was learning to work as a group of ten as opposed to a group of five. Alan and Debby explain, "We were always counting everyone whenever we went some place!"

Debby and Alan had always been active with their birth children. They spent time swimming, bike riding, and picnicking. But those activities slowed down for a period of time as the family adjusted to their increased ranks. "It took us a while to adjust to each personality," Debby says. "Our three kids were older, so it took time to adjust to small children again...and changing diapers!"

Soon the family realized that in order to blend together they had to do things together. Now they're back to family outings at the local swimming pool. Lazy Sunday afternoon picnics returned. As soon as Matthew and Christopher were old enough, bike riding was incorporated into the family routine once again.

Another long-standing family tradition involved one parent and one child spending a Friday evening together, away from the house. Debby and Alan take turns each week treating a different child to a night out. The kids look forward to their night alone with either Mom or Dad. They say it gives them a chance to spend quality time with each other. The time provides each child with an opportunity to open up to their parents.

Though Matt, Jenny and April were in favor of the adoption, they didn't realize how difficult it would be to accept five little brothers and sisters into their lives. Suddenly an allowance that was split among three was now divided among eight. "We just had to keep reminding them of their commitment," Alan says.

At the same time, Jamie, Joshua, Michaeleen, Matthew, and Christopher had their own adjustments to make. Because they had been separated and lived in different foster homes, it took some time for them to blend together again. To complicate matters, the children had been moved and lived in several foster homes. It took some time for them to realize they had found a permanent family with Alan and Debby.

All eight children needed time to understand and know one another. "After a honeymoon period, we had to deal with sibling rivalry," Alan remembers. "In a way, it was like blending three families into one." Time, patience, and learning not to over-react helped the family get through the tough times. "We try to keep things simple," Debby explains. "We have three rules. Obey Mom and Dad. Don't lie. Mom and Dad will always love you." Both Alan and Debby reinforce this message with hugs, kisses, and tickles.

Emotional and financial support from their relatives, their church, and their school has been a tremendous help to Alan and Debby. For instance, anonymous donors provided clothing and paid a semester's school tuition.

The adoption "actually made us a better family," Debby said. "We all learned to communicate better with one another. We've become a close group and the kids are very protective of one another."

Gazing at eight bright-eyed, smiling faces says it all. There is enough love to go around for all eight.

Now They Have Found Me and I Am Home

First published in *Heartlines* February 1988

Late one cool October evening in 1986 Pat and Mike White watched the news on Channel 11 in Colorado Springs, Colorado. They saw three-year-old Joseph featured. They looked at one another and knew this child was meant to be their own. Pat spoke to a volunteer in the office of The Adoption Exchange and the couple soon began the home study process and their journey to adoption.

The following January, Joey went home with the Whites. Although the White's five-year-old son Mikey wasn't expecting a little brother who could already walk, talk, and play with his toys; Joey was greeted warmly. A year later the boys were so close they often tell people they're twins.

When Joey first came to the White family, they were informed that he was probably retarded. Pat and Mike realized he would need speech and occupational therapy, and were warned that he might not bond to the family. Family therapy was recommended for several years. When he arrived, Joey could not walk up a flight of stairs and his muscle tone was poor.

Joey's progress in less than a year surprised almost everyone. His preschool teachers said his speech was better than some children without disabilities.

Although his fine motor skills still needed work, he colored a bright Christmas card for the television anchor who first broadcast his story. A bounding bundle of energy, Joey now races up stairs, wrestles with his Dad, and rides a two-wheeler with small training wheels.

Pat and Mike wish more people would adopt waiting children. They had been warned against adopting a child with special needs, but they believe that love and care with a forever family can make a difference.

Perhaps the happiness experienced by Joey and his family can best be expressed by a song he sings to his brother Mike at bedtime:

When I was born, I was lost

And Mom and Dad and Mikey couldn't find me.

They'd been looking and looking for me,

And finally they found me.

Now they have found me

And I am home.

Which Ones Are Yours?

By Suzanne Dosh, MSW,
VP of Programs for The Adoption Exchange

I could tell something was wrong when my nine-year-old daughter walked in the door at the end of the school day. She mumbled a brief "Hi" and went straight to her bedroom. After a bit of encouragement, her tears and halting words revealed the depth of her hurt feelings and confusion. On the playground her best girl friends had asked why her "real" mother had "given her away." Despite hearing her birth mother spoken of in nothing but positive terms at home, as well as knowing her birth mother cared for her so much that she made sure her child would grow up in a family who would value and love her, my daughter felt challenged and defenseless. And, not surprisingly, she was wondering what, indeed, was so wrong with her that she was so unlovable that her birth mother did not "keep her."

As an adult my daughter let me know how difficult it was for her in elementary school when the teacher gave her students the oft-used Family Tree exercise. I learned that my daughter had asked the teacher what she should do because she did not have the names of her ancestors to fill in the branches of her tree. Understandably the teacher told my daughter to use the names of her adoptive family members, but it seems she did not understand why the assignment might cause my daughter to feel unprepared for handling an activity which once again caused her to feel different. Cognitively she already understood that she had birth relatives unknown to her yet part of her. But she needed to have her different life experience validated rather than seeming to deny its existence. As she described this event, I could see that the memory still bothered her twenty years later.

Do we think about the language we use when we talk about adoption? Do we realize how we shape society's values about our children with the words we choose? How do we help our communities value adoption as a first-rate option to build a family? Do we remember how much we influence our children when they overhear how we introduce them and respond to the questions of strangers about our families? When my children were growing up, often interested persons would ask "Which ones are yours?" My response was always "all of them" rather than "he's adopted, she's a foster child, he's my stepson, and this one's mine." The first answer is entirely accurate and, more importantly, reaffirmed for my children that they are equal in my heart. The second answer provides private information for a stranger that is not any of his or her business, even if the question is well-intended. Those persons who become friends will learn the story of our families as our relationship unfolds.

Even though the finalization of an adoption is a one-time event, its impact is life-long as adoptees integrate and actualize their unique experiences during each developmental stage. We, their families, also are changed immutably as we travel this exceptional journey together. As adoptive parents and adoption professionals, let's lead the way by using sensitive and thoughtful language as we interact with our children and our communities.

Suzanne Dosh, MSW, is the VP of Programs for The Adoption Exchange and the mother of seven children by birth and adoption.

"I'm adopted!

That's when you have the same family

but not the same face."

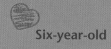

Six-year-old

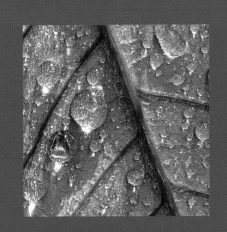

Justin and Tiffani; Shannon; Jacob

A Present for Me

We go to Aunt Virginia's every year for Thanksgiving!" There is power in that sentence, spoken by ten-year-old DeShawn just months after his adoption. Already he claims the pride of belonging. Someone expects him. It's almost like Aunt Virginia has been waiting for him every year and he is finally going to be there. DeShawn needs to create memories and tell family stories, just like other people do.

Holidays and family vacations hold a reservoir of meaning. Traditions vary from family to family. Families celebrate varying holidays. But the psychological importance is that people grow up marking important events in their lives. Birthdays, Thanksgiving, New Year's, Christmas, Hanukkah, Mother's Day, Father's Day, and graduations bring the family together to mark an occasion or a developmental milestone.

Stable, loving families look at old video tapes and photographs, play games, watch a favorite television show, or football game. They touch things that are familiar to them, eat certain foods and repeat customs that help them feel affirmed and confirm that they have a place and a basic social unit where they belong. Everyone needs history. It provides a renewed sense of identity and acceptance.

Even adults want to be a little bit frivolous and maybe even self-indulgent on a holiday. They want to dream a little and believe in magic. Mostly they want to be with people they love.

Children without parents miss all of that. This year there will be siblings who are separated when their birthdays roll around. They'll be sitting at someone else's table and someone else's mother will try to celebrate with them. Without family traditions, they grow up without threads that hold their personal identities intact. Their names aren't on anyone's holiday cards. They lose out on the intimacy of giving and receiving specially chosen gifts. Without someone to keep the stories alive they begin to forget who they look like. Instead of hearing the stories of how cute they were when they were little or laughing at the memory of something silly they did, displaced children try to get in step with someone else's customs, only to be moved and repeat the process.

The children tell us that the worst part about growing up in foster care is the loneliness. As the winter holidays draw near, The Adoption Exchange receives phone calls from well-meaning people who look for a way to give. Not long ago a group called to offer to decorate and fill shoe boxes with things like socks, tooth paste, and shower soap for several children. I felt sad. Regardless of how beautifully the boxes are decorated, those essential items aren't going to take away loneliness. The gift givers will get together, fill those boxes with pencils, crayons, and underwear; and deliver them to our office. Then they'll go home, hug their children, eat too much, walk the dog, and open gifts that represent extravagances and tender thoughtfulness. I don't want decorated shoe boxes for the children. I want them to have their very own moms and dads who will gripe at them when they forget to say thank you. I want them to have stuff they don't need, the latest toys that make them feel just like all the other kids at school.

In the Utah Office of The Adoption Exchange, staff works with volunteers and state caseworkers to "sub for Santa." In 2006 they shopped and wrapped gifts for more than fifty children in foster care, hoping to convey the message that they are not forgotten. One caseworker said, "This is the first year that Daniel has ever gotten gifts that were purchased especially with him in mind. And he is really doing well emotionally right now." The power of belonging can't be under estimated, even if the child only matters to a stranger.

The days leading up to a holiday are stressful for these children. They wonder who, if anyone, will remember them this year. They wonder if they matter. Nightmares bring back memories of past holidays that were ignored. They remember holidays marked with broken promises. They remember when excessive alcohol or drug use consumed the available cash and may have taken the place of a family meal or gifts. At times violence was part of the old tradition. These children need to heal from the scars of disappointment.

They don't connect with the excitement of holiday shopping, trips to visit with out-of-town family, or going to see Santa. They haven't helped decorate holiday treats, put up Christmas trees, or celebrated in church. They have learned to manage their fears and loss with a "don't care" attitude as a form of self preservation.

Some adoptive parents add a new holiday to their customs when their adopted children enter the family. They may call it "adoption day" or "got-cha day" and they mark the day each year to remember and celebrate. Some children don't much like being reminded that they came into the family in a different way, but none of them object to being made to feel loved or reminded that their presence is special.

Emily had lived in twenty-seven foster homes by the time she was three. Her new family celebrated her adoption as her birthday. It comforted her when her new mother told her "even though we don't have the same blood, I am part of you."

Mary relates how her son Ray slowly became integrated in the family through annual traditions and celebrations. Ray had difficulty attaching to the family because he had been in ten foster homes and a children's residential treatment facility by the time he was six and a half.

His first Easter when the family talked about the Bunny coming Ray related, "When I was at the Children's Home the staff said we were so bad the Easter Bunny wouldn't come to us. I was awake that night and saw the staff bringing in baskets because the Bunny didn't show up."

This comment crystallized Ray's dilemma for Mary. She suddenly understood he did not get excited about Christmas gifts because they might be gone the following week if he was moved to another placement. If he received a gift for his birthday it was probably taken by an older child in the foster home or that he was a child so bad that even the Easter Bunny wouldn't show up.

In this chapter the Jackson family, and adopted child Emily talk about developing family traditions that build consistency so everyone feels like they belong.

Emily's Story

First published in *Heartlines* Spring 2003

On the night before her adoption was finalized, Emily's new aunt and uncle gave her a Cabbage Patch Kid doll, complete with its own "adoption papers." Emily brought Chrissy with her to the courthouse the next day and remembers that when the judge shook her hand, Emily asked him to shake Chrissy's hand as well. This is her story.

Every year we celebrate my adoption as my birthday. On March 17, 1985, I was adopted. I was four and a half-years-old. Twenty years ago I was in one of the twenty-seven foster homes I lived in by the time I was three-years-old. The Adoption Exchange helped me find a permanent home. I was even a *Wednesday's Child*. They worked with my social worker to find a family that wanted to adopt me. By the time I was adopted, I had been diagnosed as "failure to thrive." At four and a half, I weighed only twenty-two pounds. I have no doubt that if I had not been adopted I wouldn't have made it. I remember living in foster care and wishing I had a real family. I don't have any good memories from the time before I was adopted. When you are in foster care, you never know where you are going to be next. When I was adopted, that changed. I always knew where I would go to sleep at night.

I remember meeting my adoptive parents for the first time. I walked down a long hallway holding someone's hand and entered a room where my parents were waiting. I was scared and skittish, but my Dad started playing hide and seek with me and that made me feel safe because it was fun. My mother always tells me that even though we don't have the same blood, I am part of her. We are very close - she is my best friend. The Adoption Exchange helped us find each other and I believe that saved my life. Everybody needs a family - otherwise you are lost. Your whole life is lost.

Emily is currently in college and wants to pursue a career that will allow her to make a difference in the lives of vulnerable children. She feels strongly that the children waiting in foster care today deserve a family. "So many families just want babies," she said, "but the older kids need their love even more." When asked what advice she would give to waiting children, Emily smiled. "Keep your head up," she said. "There is someone out there for you."

The Jackson Family Holiday Letter

By Alicia Jackson

December 8, 2006

Dear family and friends:

There are many star constellations in the sky, all beautiful and unique in their own way. Believe it or not, all stars have a history or an origin and it is just finding a certain star and obtaining its story that makes the sky look so beautiful. There is one very important star that we all have heard of and that is the Christmas star that appeared above the manger when the Savior was born. This star is a symbol of Christ's birth. It was seen everywhere.

It is said that when you wish upon a star it makes no difference who you are for anything your heart desires will come to you. We have come to appreciate this statement very much these past few years as our family has had quite a few dreams come true. This Christmas wish began a couple years ago when a six-year-old boy had a pretty large Christmas wish. He only wanted to have a family, but most of all a forever family. We have come to learn for ourselves that the sky is the limit, it doesn't matter what we do as long as we have each other. You have probably heard our new motto, "Ten for Eternity." We began saying this last March when all ten of us went to the temple for the last time. This saying has become very close to our hearts. Here is a little about each of us and some of our Christmas wishes.

Dad - My dad has had a busy year, from work, to home and all of the above. So he decided that he needed a break. But a week! We were all very sad when mom and dad packed their bags and went on an adventure. They spent a week on a Caribbean cruise. We missed them very much, but they had a wonderful time. Besides goofing around having fun, dad made a simple wish upon a star in order to survive being the primary pianist. He works hard and practices a lot.

Mom - Call it quits! This woman is amazing! Once again another year has passed and mom hasn't slowed down. We are finally beginning to realize that she can only be in one place at a time. From waking up at 5:00 a.m. and going to bed at 10:00 p.m. or later somehow she keeps on moving. She is the chaperone, cheer section, and cook all at once. We don't know what we would do without her. I am not exactly sure if my mom has one particular Christmas wish this year or not, but if she did I could only assume one thing and that is not to explode into a million pieces. That wouldn't be good. But in the end, her wish in a life time finally came true this year when we went to the temple with Austin so the entire family could be together forever.

Alicia - Once again writing this year's Christmas letter. Who knows what my dad would do without me! I love writing and call me crazy but I have fun doing it. My Christmas wish came along a little earlier this year when auditioning for encore choir at the high school. Out of twenty-two girls and five spots, I made it and love it. I am particularly excited about our end of the year trip to New York City and Washington, D.C. We will be going to Broadway workshops and singing at the memorials in D.C.

Megan - Go. Fight. Win. There are no simpler words to describe her. She is still hard at work doing what she loves most cheerleading. She has had straight A's all the way through middle school now and her wish is to keep it up so she will be named to the straight "A" honor roll at the end of her middle school years. Still a huge animal lover she has had an exciting time potty training her dog, Milo. Although she is extremely busy she always takes time for her dogs. She works hard at everything she does and never gives up.

Brandon - Without a doubt there is no crazier kid around. He does let his consumed energy out every Tuesday and Thursday when he has karate. He has been working hard at it and is currently an Orange belt. His Christmas wish is to be ready for his next karate belt test in January. Hard at play and slacking on work definitely describes Brandon. He loves playing with his friends and spending one-on-one time with the play station or Xbox. Although he hates his school work, he still manages awesome grades.

Ashley - Busy, busy, busy. School, dancing, singing and gymnastics this little girl has got it covered. She showed us who she truly was this year for Halloween, as a cowgirl. She definitely is a small town kind of girl. Ashley loves playing with all of the kids in the neighborhood. She loves going to school where her favorite time is lunch and recess. If you were to ask me, Ashley's Christmas wish this year is to have more hours in a day in order to accomplish everything she wants to do.

Jocelyn - All smiles and giggles. This one surprisingly takes after Brandon. She goes to school all day and still comes home with so much energy. Jocelyn is in all-day kindergarten and her favorite part is riding the bus to school. She always reminds us about family prayers and scriptures every night, just because she knows it will put off having to go to bed for a few more minutes. What can you do, except smile and go along with it. Her wish is to finally be big and get to stay up late.

Krissy - She loves being the oldest at home during the day. She has definitely assumed the role. She now realizes that if she tells Sabrina or Austin what to do they listen to her. She has found her first true love. Our new neighbors across the way have a little boy her age named Zach. She tells us that when she grows up she is going to marry him. Krissy always looks forward to Monday and Wednesday so she can go to preschool (with Zach). She is very smart for her age

and keeps learning more. Her wish is to finally be able to ride the bus to school like all the other kids.

Sabrina - A tough year. She finally decided that she wanted to be a big girl and wear panties but she doesn't like to slow down in order to use the toilet. She is always looking up towards her older brothers and sisters and sometimes it can get a little annoying. She is going through a stage of copying everything we do. She always has a smile on her face and will not go to sleep until everyone has given her a goodnight kiss. Sabrina's Christmas wish is to be a good big sister like all of her older sisters.

Austin - Spoiled rotten and loving it are the right words to describe this little kid. He is the youngest and he is by far the loudest. He has learned many things this year, but the cutest is when he runs down the hall just to keep up with the little girls. This little boy is learning lots of new words, but under the influence of my dad, the one he uses the most is "ice." He loves my dad's ice machine and would eat it all day and all night if you let him. If you're ever in a bad mood take one look at this child and he'll put a smile on your face. Austin's favorite new thing is Elmo. Wherever he goes he is always carrying his Elmo. Because of this, Austin's Christmas wish is to be able to watch Elmo 24-7.

Although our Christmas wishes this year may be simple and seem like no big deal when pieced together they make something of great importance.

When wishing upon a star in the sky, we have set goals and dreams that we want to achieve. Through hard work and determination this year we can all become something more.

In order to leave our mark this Christmas we have taken our family motto and formed our own constellation in the sky - a big "10" in the heavens. It may be tiny and hard to see right now, but we assure you that it is there. We hope that all of you can find your own constellation in the sky and make a goal as we have to reach for the stars. Remember that when you wish upon a star your dreams come true.

May God bless you and your family as he has blessed us in our hopes and dreams this Christmas season.

Love,
The Jackson Family

Jamie Jackson and his wife Sherrie, had two children, but when they couldn't conceive any more they turned to adoption. In the past three and a half years they have adopted six children. All of the children share the same biological parents.

When they started classes for adoption they said they would like three children. The workers asked if they would consider four. They agreed and were given four shortly after completing their home study. Shortly after they were told the mom was pregnant with a fifth and they agreed to take that child as well. The same thing happened the next year as well and along came child number six.

A Special Present

By Mary Bearman

Families are created and configured in many ways … but the only important way is through love. We started out as individuals and ended up as a family. This is the story of our journey to love.

The phone rang. It was Ray asking what Bob might like for Father's Day. Ray is our oldest and is now the first child to call and make plans for family celebrations. This has not always been the case. I was flooded with memories and a swirl of emotions as I looked back on the early days.

Our life teachers come in many forms. Mine came in the form of a little boy with jet-black hair, big brown eyes and a smile that could light the room. Ray was placed in our family in September 1977 at age 6 and a half. He joined Katie, almost five years old, Teddy, two-years old, my ex-husband Michael, and myself. It was unusual, even in 1977, to place a child older than the existing children in the family. Today, it is simply a placement that would not happen. Looking back, it is another affirmation to me that we do end up in the families where we truly belong; whether we get there by birth or if parents and children journey to find one another.

Ray's life history read like a Dickens novel. He was put into foster care at age two by his teenage birth mom, who was unable to care for him. Between age two

108

and 6 and a half he had been in ten foster homes and a children's residential treatment facility. I knew very little about children who suffered such trauma. My belief at the time was if you just loved a child enough everything would turn out all right. It was a belief that I was to question for years. I had thought that Ray's adoption would be the happy ending for all of us. In truth, it was the beginning of a journey that would change us forever. It was a path that included years of hard work and sometimes pain and darkness punctuated by flashes of greatness and growth, light and joy.

When Ray first arrived, he suffered from night terrors, so just getting him to sleep was an issue. He would run through the house fighting demons on a nightly basis. One night, I had positioned myself on the couch to intercept him as he came down the stairs. Teddy, still a baby, was crying that night. I watched in amazement as our newest son came down the stairs, went to the kitchen and fixed a bottle. Even though Ray had not experienced it for himself, he instinctively knew that if a toddler was crying in the night, somebody ought to care for him. Watching him take the bottle upstairs to his little brother, taking a sip or two himself, was the seed that gave me hope that this child had a heart that could still open.

However, Ray who had been so hurt in the past had trouble trusting. His experience had been that either people leave him or he is sent away. He did not believe he was really home for good and spent a great

deal of time testing. It was less painful for him to not attach to us than to open his heart to being hurt again. It was hard to know what to do to help him. If, indeed, it takes a village to raise a child, Ray's village was extensive. There were so many who cared and wanted the best for Ray. There were so many teachers that went above and beyond, neighbors who offered respite and community, mental health practitioners, friends and family support all cradled us. We had a wonderful therapist, Dr. Vera Falhberg, and the people at Forest Heights Lodge who helped keep the placement together through difficult times. The only people Ray was willing to trust unconditionally in the beginning were his new grandparents, Mimi and Pop Pop. Mimi would cook his favorite stir-fry meal and Pop Pop would show him how to hammer and fix things. There was an easy bond between them. They celebrated so many holidays with us that Ray began to associate holidays and celebrations with being part of a family. As with everything, it took time to heal.

Ray's first Christmas was bittersweet. He had learned to ride a two-wheel bike between September and Christmas. We had saved to buy him a "big boy bike" and couldn't wait to surprise him, but Christmas morning he just stood by the bike with no expression. I was disappointed because I wanted him to know we loved him and to be excited about his gift. We got the same response for his February birthday as he unwrapped the Star Wars toys he had asked for and wanted. His first Easter when we talked about the

Easter Bunny coming, Ray said sadly, "When I was at the Children's Home, the staff said we were so bad that the Easter Bunny wouldn't come to us. I was awake that night and saw the staff bringing in the baskets because the Bunny didn't show up."

It began to make sense that Ray's experiences with holidays and gifts were such that the bike he got for Christmas might be gone the next week when he moved to another placement; and if he was given a gift for his birthday, it would probably be taken by older children in the foster home or that he was a bad child, so bad, that even the Easter Bunny wouldn't show up. But because birthdays and holidays come once a year, it was a way of building a family that was consistent. He began to know what he could count on. Like all families we had our traditions. On Mother's Day, we usually went to brunch. The year Ray was 14 we went to an especially dressy restaurant. Katie and Teddy were dressed in preppy blazers and khaki skirts and pants. Ray's dress outfit was his best jeans, a black leather jacket with chains and studs offset by his very large, purple Mohawk. I'm sure to others we didn't look like we belonged together, but we did. We were family.

It was a difficult and devastating loss for all the children when Michael and I decided to divorce. There were many challenges being a single mother.

The first year The Adoption Exchange held its annual telethon, we all watched. Katie said, "Kids and parents need a way to find each other. Let's send our allowance to The Exchange."

The children each sent $3 and that was our family's first connection with The Adoption Exchange. When I needed a job, The Exchange hired me to create and implement "new concepts" in placing children, including adoption parties, parent educational and child match. The Adoption Exchange became a second family to us, and all of our children have been involved in some way through the years. Our youngest son, Mike, volunteered for two summers.

Ray left home after his 18th birthday. He needed time to find himself. We didn't know where he was for three years. He had graduated from the Job Corps when he wrote a letter saying he would like to reconnect with his family. The fear we would leave was gone. This time it was Ray who has left and come back. Finally, he had chosen to allow himself to have a "forever family".

Things had changed in the time Ray was gone. I had remarried a wonderful man named Bob and had added Brooke and Mike to our family. I was afraid Ray would feel displaced, but he viewed Brooke and Mike as a younger version of Katie and Teddy and was able to redo being a big brother in a more comfortable way. He was hungry for the stable loving father role that Bob provided and bonded quickly. Ray has said of Bob, "He is a man I admire and a father I can count on."

Bob would later write for his college reunion newsletter, "I am a father of five children. I always wanted a large family but never imagined that this would be the way it would be created."

We have spent many years as a family and have celebrated many birthdays and holidays. Ray is excited about the celebrations now. He is able to enjoy the gifts he is given and always brings beautifully wrapped presents and cards appropriate for each occasion. One Mother's Day, a few years ago, he gave me a beautiful card and inside had written:

You aren't the only Mother I have ever had, but you are by far the best mother anyone could every have hoped for. Thank you for being my Mom.

Love, Raymond.

I cherish it with all the other loving expressions Ray has sent through the years. They add another layer of healing.

When Dixie Davis was presenting a national award to honor our therapist, Dr. Vera Fahlberg, she asked Ray for input. He said lovely things about Vera and then as an aside said, " Dixie, could you tell Vera my family is very important to me now and we are close. Can you tell her that I grew up to be a good person? I think she would want to know."

I am proud of Ray. He has grown into a fine man. He is a hard worker, a good musician and a caring and loving person. He has created a good life with a lovely young woman and they love and adore each other. I am proud of all of us. I wish I had trusted that we would get to this place and hadn't spent so much time being worried and fearful. In the end, it turns out that love is enough to open a heart. In fact, it is the only thing that is enough.

It is said, "One word frees us of all the weight and pain of life; that word is love."

Our family continues to grow and to heal. Perhaps that is what family is after all, someone to stand beside you and take your part, someone to stand behind you and cover your back and some to take turns standing in front to show the way.

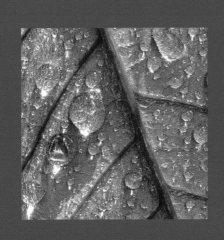

Fox Family; Arianne; and Grafton-Wright Family

Feeding the Hunger

Imagine being a child and entering a new home for the first time. Many children aren't accustomed to a family ritual that includes sitting down for a meal together. They don't know where to sit or how to act. Plates are carried to the table. But this food looks and smells different than anything they've had before.

A Utah boy attended a formal dinner and wondered if the salad he was served was his whole meal. Someone else at the table ordered a vegetarian dish piled high with green stuff. His eyes revealed his terror and disappointment. Another boy thought his adoptive mom was making "urinated salad." It was really marinated bean salad. As children integrate into a new family, the kitchen table becomes a place of fear and the battleground for power struggles.

Children who have been abused, neglected, and moved around suffer from all kinds of hunger. They eat to fill an emptiness deep inside. Jana was shocked when her daughter Germaine told her that before she came to her she would sometimes crawl on the carpet looking for food.

Hoarding and gorging are not unusual. Children hide food under a mattress to make sure they will always have something to eat. One dad kept his refrigerator full. His new teenaged son walked into the house, opened the refrigerator, and feasted his eyes on the supply. Another mom showed her new children what they could have anytime they wanted. These simple acts help tear down barriers lodged deep in the soul.

Families bond together at the table. Birthdays and new rituals help ease the sense of discomfort that children face in new situations. The Crowe family's make-your-own-dessert-night helped create memories the children used to form attachments. And there's nothing like a birthday cake with your own name on it to make you feel special and included.

Jana said, "We have adopted six children and all of them like to eat a lot. So food is important in our family with the children often cooking too. Whoever cooks gets to taste the food for 'poisoning' and gets a round of applause at the table. When our daughter was three she prayed, 'Dear God, Thanks for the food. Sometimes its good and sometimes it's not. Amen.'"

Adoption is the gift of hope for the future. Jana said another of her children wants to drive a trash truck and drink coffee when he grows up. As Bob says of raising his two adopted boys, "It takes a lot of love and a lot of pizza."

In this chapter Jana, Chris, and Brian share more stories about food, family and teaching children values.

"Make-Your-Own-Dessert" Night

This story originally appeared in the
Voices of Adoption Cookbook

B rian and Chris have provided care to children in the foster system for several years and to date have adopted six. Lea was one of the foster children. Chris saw her role (or so she thought) as a foster mother to let the children come and go while supporting the process of recruiting an adoptive family. Lea appeared on *Wednesday's Child* and was placed with a family who decided after several months that they couldn't be her parents. Through the hurts, Lea agreed with her social worker that it would be good to return to the Crowe Family home while everyone "regrouped" and a permanent family was found. She never left and her adoption was finalized in 2005.

This couple continues to adopt children in their home who become legally free, and they continue to work collaboratively with the birth families for those children who will return home. At last count Brian and Chris' children were: Lea, age fourteen; Vanessa, age fourteen; Ashley, age thirteen; Isaiah, age six; Eli, age six; Jeremiah, age five; and Tia, age two.

Chris says, "Make-your-own-dessert-night is our most favorite thing." Each week when Chris does the grocery shopping, she watches for items on sale: pretzels, Oreos, marshmallows, ice cream topping, all kinds of sprinkles, and fruit. "Each child gets his own individual plate. No one has to share or take turns or be sure what they do pleases the others (the way you do when you put icing on a cake that everyone will share.)" Chocolate almond bark is heated to dipping consistency. Everyone has a dipping bowl and a plate and creates his own dessert. "It doesn't matter if someone drools or licks the plate, because it's his own creation," she says. Chris adds, "As with all things, it is important to look past the mess."

Matters of the Heart

By Jana Zinser-Fox
First published in *Heartlines* Spring 2003

John and I have eight children; with all the love, joy, and bickering that implies. We have three big kids in their twenties: Christin, Matt, and Tim. Germaine is fourteen. Leslie and Branden are eleven. Josh is seven and Conner is five. With eight kids, there is some child mad at us at all times and there is some child hugging us at all times. These are the matters of the heart. This is our journey.

I was with my father when he died. He taught me one last important lesson with his passing. When his great and glorious life gently lifted from this earth, my father was gone, but his body remained. I realized my connection to my father was not his biology, but his personality - his spirit and soul. Families connect souls and that outlasts biology.

When we met our two little girls in their foster home, Germaine was five and Leslie was three. They came running out to meet us. Their social worker said, "Do you know who these people are?" Leslie threw open her arms and yelled, "Our family." That day, our souls connected.

Once at a gas station we stopped and opened the door. A man walked by. Leslie's joy could not be contained. She yelled from the back seat to him, "Guess what? I'm de-dopted."

Leslie and Germaine would play up the street at their friend's house, but they'd come home every now and then just to make sure we were still there.

Our kids had to figure out the family relationships. One night, picking up food at the KFC with her Daddy, Leslie said to the person taking the order, "You're talking to my mommy's husband, you know."

When the girls were asked what the best thing about being adopted was, we expected them to say their parents. But no, they both said it was getting a little brother. Joshua was three-months-old when he joined us. One day I heard the girls talking to Josh in his crib. They said, "Its safe here. We know. We've been here awhile."

When Joshua's social worker came to visit him, Leslie, afraid he would be taken from her, held on to his legs. When the social worker picked Joshua up, Leslie came, too, hanging on to his ankles for dear life. Leslie said to the social worker, "He stays." The social worker smiled and put Joshua down. Love is too precious to let go.

One day I heard someone ask three-year-old Josh if he was adopted. "Yes," he said proudly. "I was a dolphin."

When we visited Conner in his foster home for the first time, he was almost one. The social worker warned us not to expect too much. She said he would not come to us. He would scream. He was very fearful.

We walked in. Leslie and Josh sat down beside him. Conner stared at them. Then he leaned in and kissed Leslie, a kiss of hope and trust. He was with his family. Our souls connected.

We just recently added Branden to our family. We met him at an Adoption Exchange party this summer and we decided we couldn't live without him.

Branden brought even more laughter and fun into our family. His journey with us has just begun.

For all families there are struggles, disappointment, worries, and challenges. Isn't that what life is? Isn't that why you have parents?

My girls lived in an all black urban neighborhood. When they came to live with us in our predominately white suburb, we faced some cultural differences.

One day Leslie lined up the drink coasters, found two sticks, and began to bang on them, making up nonsense words to sing. She banged and sang. When she was done she said to me, "Now you try it, mom." I sat down and banged. I repeated her nonsense words. With quite an enthusiastic flourish, I ended my set.

Leslie looked at me sadly. She patted my arm. "That's okay, mom. It's hard for white girls to do."

One day Germaine was looking for her lost Ken doll. She said, "Mom, have you seen my white boy?"

There are things that happened to our children that we weren't there for. Experiences we can't fully understand. Holes left to be filled in.

Germaine told me when she was little, before she came to us, she would sometimes crawl on the carpet searching for food. When she saw my shocked face, she said, "Don't worry, mom. I gave Leslie some."

Our children had to learn the rhythm of our family. When the girls first came to us, whenever Leslie got in trouble, Germaine would hover nearby, afraid that I was going to hurt Leslie. I would tell her, "Its okay, Germaine, Leslie just has to sit here for a minute in time out." A few weeks later, I knew Germaine was relaxing, feeling more comfortable, because when Leslie did something wrong, Germaine danced around and yelled, "Put her in time out, mom. Put her in time out."

One day Leslie wanted to watch a movie, but I asked her to come and play with me. She looked up at me and said, "Do some parents make their kids play with them?"

We teach our kids honesty. Leslie bowed her head at dinner. "Dear God, thank you for the food. Sometimes it's good and sometimes it's not."

We teach our children values. Germaine had chores to do to earn spending money. She asked me, "But if I'm too tired to work, will I still get paid?"

Our kids learn to help each other. One night, over the baby monitor by Conner's crib I heard a little desperate baby voice, "May Day, May Day, calling Mommy." I ran into Conner's room and all four kids were in the crib laughing.

Adoption is the gift of laughter, seeing through a child's eyes. While playing dress-up one day, Leslie told her sister, "Germaine you pretend you're the mother and I'll be the daughter frustrated with Dad."

Germaine said, "Okay. But I'm rich and my husband is poor."

"Why is your husband poor?" Leslie asked her. She shrugged and said, "Because I took all his money." Adoption is the gift of hope for the future. When Conner grows up he wants to drive a trash truck and drink coffee.

When Leslie was little she told me when she grew up she was going to wear high heels, blue lipstick, and blue eye shadow. The image was frightening. A mother's worst nightmare! I was very worried until one day Leslie saw Mariah Carey on TV with blue eye shadow, high heels and a very low-cut dress on. Leslie pointed to Mariah and said, "That hoochie momma needs some privacy."

Adoption is the gift of trust and care. Josh said to me, "Before I was born I had nobody to guard me but God. Then I was born and I had you."

One day I read one of Germaine's spelling sentences. She had written, "If I could, I would fly to Grandpa."

And somewhere in Heaven, I know he's looking down on his granddaughter and smiling, because he knows biology isn't everything. Love holds the matters of the heart that connect our souls.

"God,

if you're listening,

I really want a family."

Fourteen-year-old
foster child

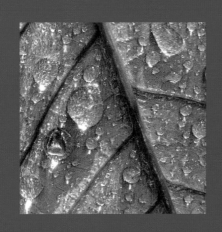

Tray and Brooke; Larkin Family; Aaron

The Next Generation

I spy Victoria soon after I walk into the room where the party is taking place. She is sitting between her mother and her grandmother eating an ice cream sundae. When she sees me coming toward her, her eyes light up and a smeary chocolate smile covers her face. She gives me a big hug and answers a couple of questions. Yes, she played golf with her grandpa this week. Yes, she is learning to swim. And yes, she has lots of friends her age. Then she returns her attention to the real attraction - her sundae — secure in the comfort of her family.

Every child should enjoy the attention and security of a loving family like Victoria. Golf probably does not matter and swimming may not be essential. But the love of the grandpa who spends his time playing with a five-year-old grandchild is important beyond words. It is grandpa's pleasure in Victoria's company that teaches her to know she has value, that she is capable. With her grandpa, Victoria is learning how to compete, to try new things, to win, and to lose. He teaches her more than how to swing a club. He is building the foundation for her self-esteem.

A simple activity like splashing in a plastic pool in the backyard with mom and a few friends seems like a normal way to grow up and it should be. Those little girls will take turns with the water hose, will make mud pies together and between the giggles will develop a bond. A few years from now, they will share secrets and have sleepovers; they will share cakes with candles to blow out as they celebrate their birthdays.

Adoption makes ordinary things possible for children whose birth families are not able to give them safety and a future with promise. Those ordinary moments are everything. Not only do they enhance the present for a child, they open up an entire future. By being loved and made to feel special from time to time, children learn they are loveable and have something to contribute to others. Given a safe environment to explore, children learn to trust themselves, to stretch, to grow, and to take reasonable risks.

The gift of a normal childhood was given to Victoria long before she was born. It was pieced together over a generation ago when Lisa, Victoria's mother, was a little girl. When it was not safe for Lisa to live with her birth family, procedures were put in place to make a plan for adoption. And that was good for Lisa. Family hikes and camping, interspersed with hugs and lots of conversation were good for her. Parents to listen to her fears and hold her through her tears helped her heal and begin to develop a sense of who she could become. They encouraged her to think she could consider going to college. With coaching and cheering, Lisa started college, changed schools, dropped out for a while, and returned to finish the work that qualified her

to become a teacher herself. Along the way, she married and has become a very good mother.

How does adoption enhance lives? Ask Lisa. But like every adoptive parent I know, her parents insist it is *their lives* that have been enhanced. They grew as they stretched to meet the challenges of a sometimes troubled adolescence. They learned to love in ways they had not known they were capable. They learned to help Lisa set attainable goals and shared the thrills of achievement. They cannot imagine their lives without her and Victoria, their first grandchild.

The benefits do not stop there. Consider the economic impact. Had Lisa remained in foster care, society would have paid the financial costs for her care. Those costs would have grown as she became a teenager. The chances are pretty good that she would have encountered the corrections system, adding more expense. Had the government raised Lisa, she may well have needed "independent living" services and there would have been no one available to help finance her college education. Chances are pretty good that Lisa would be applying for government assistance to help her support Victoria and help her train for a job.

Lisa's adoption benefited many people in her community. The ballet teacher had another pupil in her class, she and her mom shopped for stylish lenses when her eyes required correction. Lisa's playmates learned some valuable things about inclusion, love, family, and human potential as they grew up with her.

The impact of that one adoption ripples through successive decades. Adoption changes the configuration of future generations and it directly influences everyone. It influences lives in major and subtle ways.

A young man named David says that the most difficult thing for him about growing up in foster care was the loneliness. He recently told a group of caseworkers that he does not know how to make friends because he gave up on being able to stay in one place from one school year to the next as a child. He missed learning the give-and-take of ordinary relationships and still struggles to understand the principles of reciprocity, generosity, and equality that build enduring friendships. How does adoption impact lives? Ask David. He was never adopted. Now in his thirties, he is still lonely.

Nothing brings The Adoption Exchange more pleasure than the moments when one of our children, now grown, drops in to say hello. It is a thrill to meet the next generation - our children's children. Often they'll find their photographs framed and hanging on our walls. Whether they know it or not, we think about every one of them.

There may be no better way to stop the cycle of abuse and neglect than to give the child a chance to experience the love of a healthy parent. Adoption is one of the ways that society heals itself. Victoria was born into a home with uncles, grandparents, and great aunts to love her and to provide the safety net for her mom, dad and twin brothers just in case they need support.

In this chapter Paula, Marion, and Nastassja share how adoption has shaped generations.

Enjoying His Own Missed Childhood

By Paula Pickle

Jeremy was seven and a half when we brought him into our home along with his half sister who was four and a half. He was very guarded, anxious, oppositional, and passive-aggressive in his behavior. He had been in fourteen placements and had suffered most kinds of abuse you can imagine. He didn't want to do anything anyone asked him to do. At one point as a teenager, he told me he thought he was a "criminal genius" and thought he could outsmart anyone. He continued with this behavior into his very late teens.

I believe three things turned him around. We never gave up on him. He spent time in jail for "blowing off" his probation appointments. This changed his mind about the direction he wanted for his life. When I was critically ill and nearly died, he was there night and day, later telling a therapist/friend tearfully that he wasn't ready to lose me.

Jeremy has a very strong work ethic. He has been able to work in various capacities in the restaurant and banking business and is now in the mortgage industry. He married a girl who was also adopted. She has had a difficult life and does not have a close relationship with her adoptive mother, so I consider myself her mom as well. They have two sons - a three-year-old and a five-year-old. Jeremy has stated on many occasions that he will not allow his children to go through the same things he did, no matter what it takes from him.

There is nothing like a grandchild, especially when your personal parental experience includes only adopting older children from child welfare. A grandchild provides a glimpse into the sweetness and acceptance of a child who has not been damaged by life's experiences. What a treasure! It is enough to make your heart swell and tears come into your eyes to watch your son being the father you often questioned would ever be possible. I watch my adopted son with his two boys and it is as if he is enjoying his own missed childhood with them. He is a committed father who wants to make sure that his children don't have to struggle as he did. And the icing on the cake is that I get to spoil these special grandchildren, then send them home!

I can describe numerous occasions where I watched Jeremy with his children. One stands out in my mind. We were at an indoor swimming pool that had a pirate ship in the middle with water slides. He didn't just help his children play on the ship. He literally went with them, sometimes climbing through portholes that I thought he might get stuck in. The joy on his face brought tears to my eyes. He was healing himself while playing with them. I've watched similar activities like raking leaf piles and jumping in them with the kids and playing in the snow with them. This from someone who as a child had difficulty "playing." I am so proud of the man he has become, and there is nothing I would rather do than watch him continue to grow into the man and the father I hoped he could be.

Paula Pickle, MSW, is Director of the Colorado Post Adoption Resource Center, a partnership of The Adoption Exchange and Colorado Department of Human Services.

Breaking the Cycle

By Marion Neiser

The Adoption Exchange introduced us to two of our three adopted children. Brent and I started volunteering at the Exchange when we moved to Colorado in the mid-1980s. Several years earlier when we lived in Kentucky we had already adopted one special needs child and we were interested in adding more children to our family through adoption.

Through The Adoption Exchange we were able to read and volunteered to help write profiles of waiting children. When I was assigned Steve's file, I called the office and asked if I really had to write it - we wanted to adopt him instead. And ultimately we did adopt Steve (age six) in 1988, and April (age ten) in 1994.

Like many families who choose to adopt older children, there are periods of discovery, therapy, coaching, and mentoring to overcome years of neglect, abuse, and abandonment. Our children also faced emotional challenges and developmental delays stemming from their tumultuous formative years.

We sought out and embraced outside resources to help our children realize that their past would not dictate their future, and that they could hope, dream, and set goals for the future like other children from more stable homes. What a joy it was to see each child eventually let go of worrying daily whether they'd have food, clothing, and safe shelter…and begin to open their hearts and minds to the bigger childhood question of "What do I want to be when I grow up?"

We were encouraged by adoption experts and social workers to establish daily and weekly routines for our family to give the children a sense of consistency in their lives. We also enjoyed planning various activities and annual family vacations with our children, to open their eyes and stir their imaginations within the world around them…and to show them what stable families do.

Fast-forward to 2007 …and it's hard to believe we've been involved in adoption for twenty-four years now! If you do the math, you'll realize that our children are now young adults. Christy is thirty-two. Steve is twenty-six and April is twenty-three. Brent and I have transitioned into the role of parenting adult children and the delight of being grandparents! Christy is the mother of Logan, age seven, and Steve is the father of Xavier, soon-to-be four.

The joy of being a grandparent is unique and wonderful in itself. The greater joy for Brent and me comes from seeing that Christy and Steve are both devoted parents to their children.

An observer would never know these competent young parents were born into painfully dysfunctional family environments. Adoption works! It's as simple as that! Given a second chance to experience healthy family dynamics, through adoption, Christy and Steve are making appropriate choices in parenting their children. They are breaking the cycle of intergenerational abuse and neglect that runs rampant in our society and makes news headlines almost every day.

Knowing we have been instrumental in re-shaping three lives, and seeing this being replicated in the lives of our grandchildren gives us a tremendous sense of satisfaction and purpose. Dixie Davis' familiar phrase 'forever family' takes on additional meaning when you think that as adoptive parents we are changing lives now—and for the next generation.

Relying on Oneself

By Jillian Hochstetler

Nastassja entered the foster care system at the age of four and was never adopted. Growing up, her mother was always very sick. Though she had great love for her daughter, she was often too sick to care for her. Nastassja was removed from her birth home after her mother noticed she had become very sick and could barely lift her head. When the emergency responders arrived they discovered that she had been eating mouse droppings to feed herself. They removed her from her home and placed her in an orphanage. Her long journey within the foster care system began.

"I was a child who grew up in the system," Nastassja says, "in an orphanage, in foster care, and group homes. Growing up I had a lot of obstacles to overcome and I feel for children living in foster care now." She remembers feeling much anxiety as a foster child waiting for her forever family, "I kept hoping it was my turn and was disappointed again and again."

Nastassja was placed in over nine different placements that she can remember. She had very few things of her own growing up. Her most prized possession was a 1977 Sonny and Cher *A Family Again* magazine. It was the one possession she kept with her as she moved throughout the foster care system. To her it was a symbol of hard work and accomplishment. She worked many hours in the corn field at one of her residential placements to gain enough money to buy the magazine. She remembers how relieved she was to find the magazine in her school locker when a social worker came to school to take her to another placement. The rest of her belongings were left behind at the group home.

At fifteen-years-old, since she had never been placed in an adoptive home, she decided it was time to stand up for herself. Nastassja stood before a judge and told him her story. With tears streaming down her face, she recounted the abuse and neglect she had experienced while being in the foster care system. She told the judge, "You wouldn't want this for your kids. I know my mother couldn't provide for me, but my mother never would have done this to me."

After hearing her story, the judge decided that the state would provide Nastassja with an apartment of her own to live in as she finished up high school. In addition to going to school full time, Nastassja worked nights at Famous Footwear and at Ice Cream Works. She worked incredibly hard because she wanted to provide for herself. She wanted to finish her education and have a normal life. "I remember I only had one fork, one spoon, one knife, one plate----but that was all I needed," she said.

Today, as a parent herself to five children, Nastassja hopes to instill in her children the value of hard work and to believe in themselves. The cover and pages of her Sonny and Cher magazine are worn with age, yet Nastassja still looks at the magazine as one of the few reminders of her childhood and as a symbol of her hard work and determination.

She saw how the opportunity to live on her own and provide for herself at a young age shaped her and today tries to instill that in her children.

Families to Be Found

In the city
There are families to be found
Scattered lavishly around
In silent places
To replace the one that's lost
By death
Or distance
Or quarrels never healed
As happens.

There is a grandmother for those who need one,
Grey-haired and gentle
With cakes to bake
And love left over - never used.
There is a grandfather for those who want one
Quiet and eccentric
With gifts to buy
And stories left over - never used.

In the city
There is blood-love
The kind that flows
When hearts expand.
There is cross-breeding
And genealogies are mended
Or improved.

There are families to be found.

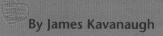

By James Kavanaugh

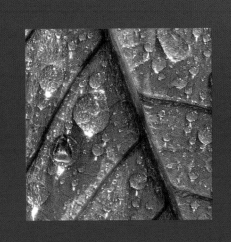

Jasmine; Cornelius; and Rodjanigue

How Old Is Too Old?

Some believe that the primary developmental task of teenagers is to emancipate. But it isn't possible to grow up and leave home, if you haven't had a home to leave. How old is too old? By the time a child is in school, society says he's too old to take naps in the afternoon or color outside the lines. He's too old for thick pencils, whining, and sucking his thumb. By the time he goes to high school, he's too old to acknowledge he's afraid of the dark. And sometimes he thinks he's too old to admit he gets lonely.

By the time he graduates, is he too old to look out at the crowd and wish he had a mom or a dad who was there to take his picture and weep with pride? When he's old enough to learn to drive, is he too old to need a frightened and nagging parent to sit in the passenger seat clutching the dashboard while screaming instructions at him? Is he too old to need someone to tell about his first important job?

When he has a baby, is he too old to want grandparents for his child? Too old to want to pick up the phone to tell grandpa what his namesake said when he bumped his head? Too old to need someone to sit with him when his son has emergency surgery?

We're surely not ready to live on our own when we turn eighteen. In the United States today the average age that a young adult becomes independent of parents is said to be twenty-six. Most parents will tell you that their children continue to need to come home from time to time well into their twenties - not just for holidays - but for a place to live while they save money for a security deposit on an apartment; when they are between house-mates; for advice or grounding; to obtain financial support for college; or when the car breaks down.

Jama is a perfect example. Social services and the courts determined that she would never be returned home when she was sixteen-years-old. Jama emancipated at age eighteen and spent a great deal of energy being fiercely independent. Eventually she reconnected with her sister's former foster family. After lots of visits, she mustered up the courage and asked them to be her family. She was nineteen-years-old when she found her own family. The adults had serious discussions about what it meant to be a family. After four years Jama described her family as "the world and then some."

How old is too old to be adopted? When does a child outgrow the need for love, stability, and the enduring warmth of a family? How old is too old for the mundane and exceptional experiences that make up normal family living? The answers are found in the eyes of the teens that wait to belong. I dare you to read the poem Annie wrote. Go ahead. There is no such thing as too old.

In this chapter adoptive parents Elizabeth, Gary, Susie, Annie, and Sheila describe the delight older children can bring to a family.

A Child Who Has Hope

Every child has a dream or a story to tell;

But some don't tell them like others do.

Some just take the pain and others give up.

But those who do put up with it don't give up their hope.

So even when the days get rough they keep on going.

When things get worse as the days go by we don't give up our hope yet.

When the pain gets worse we never give up hope.

When we feel like crying we hold each other close

And pray and keep on hoping.

And then when we almost give up our hope we are blessed

And we only remember a life we once had;

And we know in our hearts that hope lives forever!

By Elizabeth Hawkins,
age fourteen

Raising Cory: A Dad's Perspective

First published in *Heartlines* Spring 2003

Father Gary Waddingham, an Episcopal priest, had already adopted one child when he saw Cory in The Adoption Exchange's Photobook. "Cory became my son in 1989, the day after he turned fourteen," he said. "Cory had been in the system for a couple of years by the time we found each other and we have done well together. He needed a strong dad in his life." Cory is almost finished with college, works as a driver for Federal Express, is married, and has two small children. He and his wife own a home and are very close with his dad and with his wife's family.

"Adopting changes your life," Gary said. "Your whole extended family can be enriched by this child that enters the picture. When you become a parent, whether of an adopted child or a biological one, life changes. It defines who you are. The important thing in life is that your child, and someday their children, are waking up every morning and breathing. It expands your world outside of yourself and your own worries."

When asked what advice he would give to a new adoptive parent, Father Waddingham says, "Take it one day at a time. You don't need to deal with everything all at once. Part of having children is not having everything defined. Remember that they are people in their own right. And that's a wonderful thing."

Elizabeth Finds Her Way Home

First published in *Heartlines* Fall 2002

We were not looking to adopt. My husband, Greg Hawkins, was heavily involved in a race for the United States Senate and we already had twelve children. One day as we were watching the local news, *Wednesday's Child* came on. At the end of the clip with newscaster Shauna Lake, a bright eleven-year-old named Amelia announced that when she grew up she hoped to be a teacher or a lawyer. My husband (a teacher and a lawyer) looked at me and whispered, "Call and find out about her." With a string of miracles, God's grace, the help of wonderful social workers, and the supportive child advocates at The Adoption Exchange, we adopted our new daughter - now called Elizabeth. Her story could fill a book. A book with a happy ending.

Our experience can be summed up in one word, "GRATEFUL!" Kathy said, "Grateful for those foster parents and workers who really care about the children they serve. Grateful for agencies like The Adoption Exchange who keep the needs of children in the public eye. Grateful for the sacrifices of our other children that has made this adoption possible. And grateful to Elizabeth who has willingly worked to do her part to make our family work."

The World...and Then Some

First published in *Heartlines* Spring 2000

An Emergency Medical Technician drove home one evening from visiting with her parents and came upon a horrible car accident. Many other passers-by were at the scene, but only she was professionally trained to handle this situation. She worked on both victims and managed the scene until the ambulances came. She knew the twelve-year-old girl would not make it - her head injuries were too severe. It was unclear if the sixteen-year-old would survive. She was conscious and afraid. The EMT talked to her and soothed her. She continued to manage the scene until both girls were taken away in ambulances.

After being interviewed by the police office, she got into her car to go home. Suddenly, she realized the magnitude of what had just occurred. She turned around and drove back to her parent's house. When she walked through the door, her mom and dad saw the blood all over her clothes and the exhaustion, fear, and sadness in her eyes. They comforted her while she cried and told her story.

Families are a vital support in our lives. This need does not go away when we become adults. The parent-child relationship simply evolves into a different kind of relationship - with different dynamics. Each year

25,000 young people in our foster care system will emancipate - or leave the system - when they turn eighteen with no permanent family to call their own.

By the time these young people are "cut loose" by the Child Welfare system, they often lack the skills and resources to provide for themselves. Statistically, only fifty percent exit the system with a high school diploma, fewer than half are employed, twenty-five percent have been homeless, and two to four years after leaving the system, less than one in five are completely self-supporting. As adults, they often experience challenges with forming trusting, lasting relationships. Relationships have only caused pain for them thus far and they certainly do not last.

Approximately one quarter of the children in care have no plans for either being reunited with their birth families or of being adopted! Why does this happen when the injustice of it to young people, and to our society as a whole, is so abundantly evident?

Placement workers sometimes operate from the bias that older children don't need or want permanent families. Adolescents will often back that belief up by saying that they don't want a family (although deep down they really do). Workers and therapists don't want to risk the adolescent experiencing another rejection if an adoption disrupts. Many potential adoptive families fear adopting adolescents because of their behavioral issues and the depth of their emotional issues. Often, these children are labeled "unadoptable" by our system.

Susie and Greg committed to adopting Jessica when she was twelve-years-old. Jessica was labeled "unadoptable" by many of the professionals in her life. She had approximately fourteen moves since the age of six, including three adoption disruptions, and had challenges at school with chronic lying and stealing. When Greg and Susie met Jessica at an adoption party over three years ago, they knew they wanted to adopt her. Luckily, Jessica's worker also advocated for her adoption and despite the recommendations from other professionals to the contrary, Jessica was placed with Susie and Greg.

The couple certainly had fears. Would Jessica ever attach to them? Would she lie and steal from them? Would she hurt the family dog? What about all the "labels" and diagnoses that Jessica carried? What did these diagnoses mean for Jessica's life and for their lives? But when they looked at Jessica, what they really saw was a sweet, twelve-year-old girl with a zest and spirit for life. Jessica was placed with the Best-Keefe family at the age of twelve and legally adopted one year and one day later. She is now fourteen. In the last two and one-half years, her negative behaviors have decreased and her academic performance has improved. The family is very attached to one another. As Greg put it, despite the challenges, "it's fun!"

When Jessica was asked what she thought about all of the teens without families, she said that she thinks it's a stereotype that older kids are unadoptable. She said that when a young person lives in a group home, the focus is on behavior and that young person does not want to get close to people. Susie added that ". . . people don't know or see children's true potential through all the labeling and the problems caused by multiple moves . . . group homes are not a fair territory to judge children on whether or not they are adoptable."

"Or loveable," added Jessica.

Jama also spent many years in the foster care system. She entered the system at age twelve because of substance abuse on the part of her parents. Social services and the courts determined that she would not ever be returned home when she was 16-years-old. Her goal was switched from *reunification* with her birth family to *emancipation*. She had spent the last four years of her life in a variety of different placements, and the first twelve years of her life being neglected severely. Jama emancipated at age eighteen and spent a great deal of energy being fiercely independent - trying not to need anyone. She worked on holidays to avoid the loneliness.

One day she picked up the phone and reconnected with her sister's former foster - the Goers. Jama started to spend time with the Goers and became very close with the whole family, including their two sons. Finally, Jama mustered up the courage and asked them to be her family.

Jama was nineteen-years-old at the time she found a family for herself. The Goers responded with very serious discussions with Jama about what it means to be a family. Jama became a member of the Goers family as a result of her bravery and assertiveness and their openness and love for Jama. It only took a couple of months for her to start referring to them as "Mom" and "Dad." Jama is now twenty-two and is the EMT described at the beginning of this article. Jama describes her family as "the world, and then some."

Jessica, by the way, has some lofty dreams for her future. She plans on being a singer in a band. She even has a name for the band - *The Broken Butterflies*. When she wins her first Grammy, she said she'd save her parents for last in the list of people she thanks in her acceptance speech. After all, you have to save the most important for last.

Blood Is Thicker Than Water

Frightened and shaking I walk through the door of foster family number one.
Today is my birthday and I smile, but how I wish I could run.
They take me by the hands and lead me to my room.
Through my eight-year-old eyes I observe my tomb.
But I am growing more comfortable as every day passes.
I attend the third grade and become known as the foster child with the glasses.
They don't know that I don't sleep at night.
They don't know that every breath I take requires an eternal fight.
A horrendous day comes resulting in a burn from a diabolical flame.
At the ripe old age of ten I am losing the social services game.
My heart drops to the floor along with my dreams of becoming their daughter.
The fact stands clearly that blood is thicker than water.

Confused and shaking I walk through the door of foster family number two.
I meet them and smile, but I am unsure of what to say and do.
They take my hands and lead me to my room.
Through my ten-year-old eyes I observe my tomb.
I barricade myself in that cell as the sun rises and sets.
I cry an endless flood of tears with my pillow soaking wet.
On an unsuspecting day I hear the all too familiar phrase:
"Andrea, you will be leaving in just a few days."
Once again I am burned by that diabolical flame.
At the ripe old age of eleven I am losing the social services game.
My heart falls to the floor along with the dreams of being their daughter.
I guess I forgot that blood is thicker than water.

Bitter and tired I walk through the door of foster family number three.
My heart is racing as I wonder how this house will be.
They take my hands and lead me to my room.
Through my eleven-year-old eyes, I observe my tomb.
I slack off in school and I hardly ever sleep.
I am weighted down with the burdens of my world and the memories that I keep.
At the end of sixth grade I hear the same thing as before.
I walk into the house and see my few things packed by the door.
I have another scar from the diabolical flame.
At the ripe old age of twelve, I am losing the social services game.
My heart and tears fall to the floor along with my dreams of being their daughter.
I guess I forgot that blood is thicker than water.

Tearful and nervous, I walk through the door of foster family number four.
I work hard not to make eye contact and keep my eyes on the floor.
They take my hands and lead me to my room.
Through my twelve-year-old eyes, I observe my tomb.
I can't call the woman mom, so I'm not the daughter she wants.
I won't wear dresses and bows, so I'm not the girl that she flaunts.
I feel all alone and my heavy heart is jaded.
I am weak from no sleep and my hope has slowly faded.
Once again I am burned by that diabolical flame.
At the ripe old age of thirteen, I am losing the social services game.
My heart falls to the floor with the plans of being their daughter.
I guess I forgot that blood is thicker than water.

I walk apprehensively through the door of foster family number five.
My body feels emotionless and barely alive.
They take me by my hands and lead me to my room.
Through my thirteen-year-old eyes, I observe my tomb.

My teenage attitude and rebellion increases and the battle lines are clear.
I dangerously speak my thoughts with no inhibitions or fear.
It leads me to the news that was certain to come.
I am not sad or surprised; putting faith in them was dumb.
Another third degree burn from the diabolical flame;
One more lost round in the social services game.
I know deep down that I don't want to be their daughter.
I don't mind this time that blood is thicker than water.

Thanks to The Adoption Exchange I walk through the door
of foster family number six.
Of all the homes I've been to, this is the one I pick.
They take me not by the hands but by the heart and lead me to my room.
Through my thirteen-year-old eyes I observe the stone rolled from my tomb.
I learn more and more every day how a family should be.
I am happy that for once a family loves me for me.
I don't look for the dreaded words that have always come before.
I know that as time goes on, I will only love them more.
The burns have healed and I have extinguished the diabolical flame.
I can happily say that I have finally won the social services game.
I know for sure that I am their daughter
and they are the family I always dreamed of.
I know for sure now that blood and water are not thicker than love.

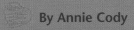 **By Annie Cody**

*Annie Patricia Cody was editor of her high school yearbook in 2006 and named one
of the "Nine Kids Who Care" (KUSA-TV) in 2005. She lives and works in Colorado,
is a frequent volunteer, and is often invited to speak on the subject of adoption.*

"Mom,

I know wherever you and Dad go,

I'll be safe."

David
age ten

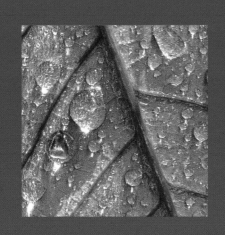

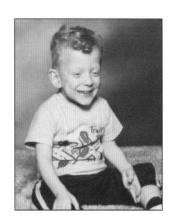

Brandon; Honeyman Family; and Trey

Ordinary People, Extrordinary Parents

It took the staff about an hour to find a family for Hope.

Claire answered adoption phone calls the afternoon a caseworker called to say that a baby had been born with disabilities so severe that the couple who had planned to adopt her changed their minds. They couldn't bring themselves to make a commitment to a baby with only a brain stem. Medical predictions were that she might live a few weeks or perhaps longer, but that she would never see, hear, speak, or respond to the love of a parent. The caseworker asked if an adoptive family could be found.

When Jackie answered the phone, Claire said, "I'm calling about a baby with disabilities that needs a family." "We'll take her," was the immediate response.

"Wait a minute. Don't you want to hear about her?" Claire asked.

"Of course. We want to know everything. But we'll take her. She's ours, no matter what the information is."

That is how Hope's relationship with her adoptive mother began. I doubt that her parents or the adoptive parents of any of the other children think they are extraordinary. But in the course of raising the children, these ordinary-looking people do extraordinary things. Like all good parents, they make a commitment to love and to do whatever is needed to help their children become what is possible for them.

Janice and Bruce said they wanted to adopt an older boy, someone healthy - perhaps like their birth son. By chance we asked them to take a look at photographs of a severely disabled three-year-old girl who hadn't begun to walk and couldn't tolerate being touched. Her files indicated she had every condition the family said they didn't want to get involved in. But she wasn't just a file. She was reality. It's a long story and a happy one. Debbie is in her early thirties now. She lived in two group homes before moving, this year, with a roommate into a 24-hour supervised apartment situation. She loves the feeling of more independence this provides. She has a part-time job which she loves in a coffee shop, and she stays busy with activities with her family, and in the community

Think about the surveys that help people select a mate. Who would accept extended family members with mental health diagnoses or criminal behavior? Now think about how the surveys are usually answered. Who really got what they asked for? Now think about yourself. If your own behavior, medical records, and family history were put in a file would anyone have wanted to pursue a family relationship with you? It's

realistic to think about limits and it stretches your limits to think about what's real.

We always encourage people considering adoption to go to the websites and look at the real, waiting children. We like to let the eyes and the hopeful smiles of the children speak. Maybe you'll be like Janice and Bruce when they called about a second adoption. I asked them if they'd consider another child with special needs like Debbie and they said, "What? You mean Debbie had special needs?"

Parents of children with special needs repeat over and over again that they see the children as a blessing and really grow because of the love they receive in return. Jackie explains it this way, "We no longer see what our children can't do, but what they can do. So many times I am asked at school staffings to list our child's needs or disabilities. I struggle to answer what is wrong with our children - they are perfect in my eyes."

Janice said, "We have been so blessed. Debbie was totally opposite of what we thought we would get, but God had a better surprise. If I only had the capacity to love, forgive and see beyond faults as she does. She has been one of my biggest teachers. My heart cannot find all the words for the feelings that well up inside of me. We love her so incredibly much."

After Debbie's graduation from high school, she moved to a group home and began an even more independent life of her own.

Janice said, "I wanted to let you know how beautifully Debbie has progressed and grown. We are so proud of her. I feel we have grown and progressed as well."

We took the "road less traveled." It wasn't always the smoothest. Some challenges were unique and some were routine. Some challenges are ongoing. She has some OCD, but her seizures are under control. She and we grew up learning together but, in the long run, we have each had a positive impact on the life of the other.

Parents Tristen and Lynne described their life with Nathan by saying that he had revived their own childhoods and taught them to see the wonder in the simple things in the world.

Unconditional love is a powerful force. It has the ability to transform both the giver and the recipient. It can make the ordinary extraordinary. It can help children live longer and achieve more than anyone ever believed possible. In this chapter Jackie, Doxie and Richard, Ellie, Janice, Tristen, and Lynee share how the adoption of special needs children has positively impacted their lives.

I couldn't look in your face

And find mine.

I couldn't see your toes, or ears,

Or smile and note a resemblance.

I couldn't look at your hair

And remember mine as a child.

In order to love you,

I had to look past all of that,

Directly into your heart.

Vicki Krausz
Adoptive Mother

A Special Family

By Ellie Valdez-Honeyman

"It drives me crazy when people think I'm a saint for adopting kids with 'significant' special needs!" I'm not sure anyone intentionally plans to adopt kids with significant needs, but when it happens, you often find rewards that you never anticipated. You also find challenges that you never imagined. We wanted a big family, but after two sons, we could no longer have birth children. We decided that foster care might fill the void. But the coming and going of children in and out of our lives was not our idea of how a family should work. After providing foster care to twenty-seven children in seven years, we decided to adopt a son who had been with us for three of his four years of life. Bob was also our first experience with a child who had significant special needs. While his issues were undiagnosed, it was evident that his development was significantly delayed in all areas…except for one…his ability to make everyone who met him fall in love with him.

After Bob, four beautiful daughters joined our family. Three of them have significant needs related to Down syndrome. By the time our two youngest children came, we were no longer spring chicks. Adoption had been such a positive experience for us that we never gave thought to the down side that our ages posed! In addition, we suffered from the American "independence syndrome" that dictates taking care of your problems and difficulties on your own. Asking for help is considered a weakness and striving for independence is the norm. Well,

155

we had an experience that convinced us that "no man (or family) is an island." We served as co-parents to twin girls for about six years. Our willingness to be involved made it easier for the blind mother to successfully parent these two little girls. It was a beautiful experience for us and one that taught us a lot.

It was this experience that "hatched" the idea of a co-parenting project. The Adoption Exchange found it intriguing that such an arrangement could prevent out-of-home placement and decided that it was worthwhile to pursue the idea for families who had adopted a child with special needs. These families could be matched with a volunteer who could provide support in parenting the child through respite, advocacy, moral support, recreation, and participation in mutual family celebrations related to the child. With supports in place, the disruptions of some adoptions might be avoided.

The project evolved into a vehicle to provide information to families about post-adoption services available to them, publication of a resource book, and the formation of a post-adoption advocacy and support group. My participation in this project was invaluable to me. Through it I found that the single most important thing to learn as an adoptive parent is that this adoption thing is not an "island" experience. It truly takes all formal and informal resources that the

"village" has to offer. I could not parent these last two daughters if it weren't for programs such as Women, Infants and Children, Health Care Program for Children with Special Needs, Medicaid, adoption subsidy, special education supports and services through the Individuals with Disabilities Education Act, as well as family support services through our county's Community Centered Board.

In 1996, Mike quit his job in a large corporation and we opened a family printing business. The printing industry has been good to our family. We hope it will continue to offer the children the opportunities to be productive, even after we are gone.

For us, adoption might be a shallow experience without the love and support of our family and community. People who can't, for whatever reason, do what Mike and I have done, are there, willing to be supports for us, and it is in this embrace that we feel most at peace. Yes, there are days when I feel more like a martyr than a saint, but most days I feel blessed to have been chosen for this wonderful adventure.

Ellie Valdez-Honeyman and her husband, Mike, live in Colorado. Five of their seven children are adopted and four of them have significant special needs. Ellie is an active volunteer in activities related to adoption and disability issues.

Jeremiah's Circles

First published in *Heartlines* Spring 2003

Jeremiah smiles and shakes his head as he looks toward his parents, Richard and Doxie, who adopted him in 1990 when he was seven-years-old. Without a hint of annoyance or exasperation, he turns to his dog and asks him with his voice to stop barking at the mail carrier who dropped a handful of envelopes into the mailbox. James, his friend and companion, continues to bark from behind a shrub despite Jeremiah's request. Jeremiah laughs at his pup with a big grin and continues to eat his lunch. A few forkfuls later, Jeremiah is making his way to the house from the picnic table in the back yard.

With his father by his side, Jeremiah slowly walks across the yard, struggling to control his body. Though cerebral palsy and developmental disabilities limit Jeremiah, they do not prevent him from accomplishing significant feats. Jeremiah beams with pride as he talks about graduating from high school in May 2003. He thumbs through his yearbook and shares stories of friends, influential teachers, and fond memories. Jeremiah talks with excitement about his second graduation, from dog training school, where he and James learned to function as a team in a world that does not always accommodate people with special needs.

Despite the daily challenges that Jeremiah must overcome and in spite of early childhood experiences full of trauma and pain, Jeremiah is a happy young man with a sincere laugh, great smile, and appreciation for life that defies his past.

Rescued from an uncertain future by his adoptive parents, Jeremiah was given a second chance to benefit from a supportive family and live in a stable, permanent home. That second chance has made a world of difference. The love of caring parents has given Jeremiah opportunities to learn, establish friendships, and develop interests. His spirit allows him to make the impossible possible, which he demonstrates each day through the simple acts of talking, eating, and dressing - tasks Doxie and Richard were told by case workers he would never be able to complete. Through his successes he inspires others around him to overcome difficulties, rise above barriers, and aspire to meet and exceed goals.

His parents, Doxie and Richard, share in his life with great pride. Though adopting Jeremiah was not a decision taken lightly, it was a decision that was easy to make. "We did it because it was beautiful and natural," they explain. "We just had so much love to give and felt there was a child who needed our love." Doxie and Richard eagerly talk about adopting Jeremiah and offer insight to families considering adopting a child with disabilities. Richard adds, "It is an honor and privilege to be part of a child's life and to this day we still marvel at him."

Doxie and Richard spend a great deal of time helping Jeremiah develop the skills he needs to gain as much independence as possible and foster Jeremiah's many interests. His bedroom is filled with model automobiles and magazines that fuel his passion for cars. Jeremiah shares his passion for cars with anyone who will listen and speaks with great enthusiasm about his favorite vehicle, a vintage Chevrolet Bellaire from the early 1960s. Though Jeremiah will likely never learn to drive, his parents have given him the freedom to express himself, never allowing the barriers that society imposes upon him to limit his imagination. His parents express this by sharing, "Our difficulty was not with Jeremiah, but rather with the roadblocks built by society."

Doxie and Richard work tirelessly to minimize those roadblocks. Through his enrollment in an enrichment program for people with special needs, Jeremiah attends cultural events, visits local libraries and museums, and has the opportunity to help others through service projects. Put him in a room with forty other people and Jeremiah immediately takes on the role of host, introducing people to one another and encouraging conversation. Soon enough all of the able bodied people in the room are following his lead. Jeremiah explains that helping others is his favorite part of the program because he likes to make others feel good. And because of the sincerity of his smile, he not only makes people feel good, Jeremiah makes people feel special.

Jeremiah, now twenty five, keeps us updated on his activities through his website www.jeremiahscircles.com.

"I'm so glad you found me.

I had something missing,"

 Malik,
victim of fetal alcohol syndrome,
speaking to her adoptive mother.

What We Were Meant to Do

By Jackie Washburn

think our love story began way before we were married but I will begin there. Tom and I met and married in Colorado Springs in October of 1976. We were both military, an older couple and desired to begin a family as soon as it was possible. Ryan was born ten months later and we were thrilled. We got transferred to Europe and were blessed with the birth of our second child, Penny. We both wanted me to be a stay-at-home mom, but I had a need to feel like I was being useful in the community so we looked into doing foster care. While stationed in Georgia we began our twenty year journey and our wonderful path to "family."

With a degree in special education it didn't take long for DSS to start calling us to foster special needs children. Both Tom and I knew from the start this was what we were meant to do, being called by God to care for his angels. We fostered over seventy children. Some we provided only overnight care and others we adopted. Each child has added to our lives beyond words. Our biological children always had many, many brothers and sisters to play with and it was never boring at holiday times!

We now have adopted ten special children and although we feel our family is not yet complete, we are happy with where we are and who we have been given. Each of our children were hand picked by both God and me to be with us to guide through life. All are treasures beyond words. All of our children have preventable disabilities. By either abuse or drugs our children are "not normal." But we have come to judge not with the standards most judge by but with our hearts. We no longer see what our children can't do but what they can do. So many times I am asked at school staffings to list our child's needs or disabilities. I struggle to answer what is wrong with our children - they are perfect in my eyes. Hope may not see, but she can hear the birds sing and her eyes flutter when the wind blows. Matthew may not be able to walk, but his smile greets me every day. Steven may not be able to speak, but I can hear him say he loves me hundreds of times a day.

I can say we don't go unnoticed in public places. Three in wheel chairs, g-tubes and tracheostomy tubes with five others in tow are hard to miss. A.J. is our bundle of energy, often running into a room first, searching for a spot big enough for all of us. We take a whole pew in church and almost empty the grocery store on shopping day. There is an endless list of things to repair or mend and the laundry never is caught up. Dinner time is loud, giggly and plates seldom match.

Tom and I may not have fancy clothes or cars or much time to read or talk, but we wouldn't trade our family for any other or for any amount of wealth. Not everyone is lucky enough to have such a crew to love. We are so blessed by each of our children I can only smile from deep inside when I even think of them. A.J. once asked if we were rich or poor and I told him we were very rich. He said he thought so because we love each other so much and we always have fun. So it is with great pleasure that I share with you this story about our family-- Ryan, Penny, Heather, Missy, Kimmy, Malik, A.J., Matthew, Steven, and Hope. Jeff and Cody are in heaven helping us find our way Home.

How Nathan Has Changed Our Lives

By Tristen Wiley and Lynn Fee

Our family is a close knit family. We love and respect each other. We support and encourage each other. We laugh and cry with each other. We eat our meals at the table together. We go to church together. We're huge St. Louis Cardinals Fans. Having Nathan as part of our family is the greatest blessing we have ever been graced with.

Nathan has revived our own childhoods and has taught us to see the wonder in the simple things in the world, like watching the leaves fall from the trees, listening to the rain, watching the phases of the moon, and counting stars. We have learned that any spoon, stick, or our hands are perfect for playing drums anytime and anywhere.

We have learned to slow down our busy fast-paced lives and truly as they say "stop to smell the roses." Nathan loves trains. So we drive miles out of the way just to drive over, under, or along the train tracks. And we even try to time our arrival at train crossings so that we can see the trains. We count how many train cars go by and the different types of train cars - hoppers, gondolas, tank cars, flatcars, rack cars, piggy back cars, cabooses, and of course, the engines. What was once an annoying delay is now a source of delight and interest.

Since Nathan has been part of our family, there's been no such thing as a bad day. Rush hour traffic, report deadlines, meetings, phone calls, challenging technology, and all the things that can be frustrating during the day, simply melt away at the very sight of him.

We find ourselves being more productive at work and home. We choose projects around the house in which he can participate and plan other projects around his nap time. We are more organized and have become very diligent about germs and safety. We read food labels and are more concerned about health and nutrition.

Every facet of our lives has changed and all for the better- our health, our careers, our personalities, our hobbies and crafts, drives and ambitions, our creativity, and our imaginations. Everything we thought was good or great is now better than we could have ever hoped for.

Parenting has its challenges, but our family is a close knit family. We love and respect each other. We support and encourage each other. We laugh and cry with each other. His well-being is our life's purpose. The name "Nathan" means 'a gift from God.' And that is exactly what he is to us- a precious gift. We are humbled, honored, and blessed to be his family.

"My Mom is the best person in the world.

She loves me and adopted me so I didn't have

to grow up in foster care or be abused."

Matt
age ten

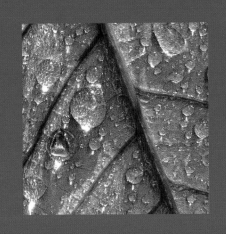

In memory of Sean
April 1, 1981 - June 14, 1996

Loss of a Child

Maybe the most important thing we can do in life is love someone with our whole heart as long as we have the time together. Early professional opinions that children with terminal illnesses should not be placed with adoptive families didn't really fit human beings, whose nature it is to love - no matter what. If Bev and Ray had listened to that questionable wisdom of others, they would have missed the joys of loving and being loved by Eseta.

Bev knew Eseta had a terminal illness when she opened her home and her heart to her. She refused to believe the limitations that physicians and educators told her would be Eseta's life. She persevered and scoured the country until she located a doctor on the west coast that was familiar with Eseta's illness.

Eseta was able to attend regular school. Her loving nature brought out the best in her parents and those around her. Eseta survived many years longer than the early predictions. Because she had a champion, more of life was possible for her than had ever been imagined.

Bev sees the situation this way. "I don't think about losing her. What I think about is all we had when she was with us."

Sean was adopted at age four and was not expected to live long. He spent eleven vibrant years at school, with his family, and was active in his community before he passed away.

As a tribute his family wrote a letter to him after his death. They said, "You are perfect now, but to us, you've always been perfect."

Mourning the death of a child includes feeling the loss of the adult he would have become. The child who has lived in a family, become a little person, or a bigger person, is imprinted on the heart of the family.

In her book, *Necessary Losses,* Judith Viorst writes that the family mourns the future expectations and the shared past, however brief.

When parents decide to adopt a child who is ill, they run headlong into the lack of understanding and sometimes outright disapproval of friends, family members, teachers and doctors. Now that the child is gone, some expect the parents' grief to somehow be less. As they see it, the burden of raising a sick child that didn't belong to the parents to begin with is gone. This limited view doesn't take into account generosity of spirit, a bonded family and the heart to accept a challenge few are prepared for.

In this chapter Sean's family, Helen, and Jackie talk about losing a child and gaining lots of love.

Solace

There was a rose that faded young;

I saw its shattered beauty hung

Upon a broken stem.

I heard them, say, "What need to care

With roses budding everywhre?"

I did not answer them.

There was a bird brought down to die;

They said, "A hundred fill the sky—

What reason to be sad?"

There was a girl whose love fled;

I did not wait the while they said,

"There's many another lad."

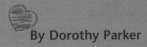

By Dorothy Parker

A Tribute to Sean

First published in *Heartlines* October 1996

In 1983 The Adoption Exchange began looking for a family to adopt Sean. He was born four weeks early, and at the age of two and a half weighed only eighteen pounds. In his first years Sean had many surgeries to correct congenital problems involving his lungs, kidneys, and stomach. His bio related that keeping food down was his biggest problem as a toddler. He ate specially pureed foods and drank milk formula containing predigested protein. Some of his problems stemmed from extensive early tube feeding, but he was struggling to speak and enjoyed playing with other children.

We said we were looking for a family who could be content with seeing him progress in small increments. We found more than that. In 1985 we found a family who loved him and cherished him just the way he was.

One summer afternoon in 1996 Sean and his parents joined us on the rooftop at Denver's Channel 4 television station for ice cream. Sean and his parents were there to help us say thanks to all of the talented people at the station who bring the very best out of the children for the weekly *Wednesday's Child* series. One of the first and longest running partnerships of its kind in the country, this relationship brings the voices and the faces of waiting children into the living rooms of millions of viewers. Sean was ecstatic to see the news anchors (whom he knew by name) and left that day with a logo hat and a big smile.

He told his mom he couldn't wait to go to school the next day to tell his friends about his tour of the station. But that didn't happen. Sean developed severe pneumonia during the night, a condition to which his severe disabilities left him particularly vulnerable. On June 14, despite the best of care, Sean died. He was fifteen-years-old. His father couldn't bear for Sean's body to be taken alone in the hearse to the mortuary. So he rode along, cradling his son's body in his arms.

A few weeks later Sean's father wrote this letter:

Dear Seanery,

Boy, are we going to miss you! You made our lives richer than we could have ever imagined. Your warm smile, quick greetings, and never forgetting a name brought joy to all of us.

Taco Bell will never be the same without you. The way you loved to sing to Jesus will be missed even during special music at church.

God used you to touch many lives, especially ours. You taught us a lot and we thank you so much. Jesus shined through you and we are so happy you are now in heaven and whole.

No more medicine...No more wheelchair...No more oxygen... NO MORE PAIN! You are perfect now, but to us, you've always been perfect. We love and miss you!

Your family

Everyone Was Crazy About Her

By Beverly Milligan

There is a reason her middle name is Joy. She was a gift from the angels. Ray and I had been foster parents for medically fragile, high risk children for a long time. We'd cared for a dozen newborn babies and four hospice clients of the county. I was emotionally drained from saying goodbye again and again. So I told the county caseworker, "I can't handle another child who is terminally ill."

But she called me anyway. There was a baby in the hospital with a rare blood disease. She was expected to live for about one year. At the time they called me, Eseta was in a body cast. Her birth mom had come into the hospital with a gun and tried to kill her. She was in protective custody, and no one was allowed to visit. She was two-months-old, and she was completely alone.

The caseworker told me that her rare disease was known in only eighteen other cases worldwide. Against my better judgment, I agreed to go see her. It wasn't easy to get into her ward at the hospital, but phone calls to the county eventually persuaded the staff to let me visit. I took one look and drove home.

I walked in the house and Ray saw the look on my face and said, "Gather up some blankets and go get her." I told the county caseworker that I could only care for her as my own child. She lived on twenty-four hour intravenous tube for a long time. And we visited medical specialists across the country, looking for treatment to extend her life. She was certainly at risk, and she was developmentally disabled. But she was my baby, and her name was Eseta Joy.

In time Eseta grew. She began walking, talking, running, playing, and dancing. There seemed to be a spiritual quality to her being, and I came to think of her as a teacher. Everywhere she went, she taught love and faith. I fought to get her into a regular classroom and the teachers at school were pretty mad at me. But it didn't last, because Eseta changed everyone's opinions about disabled children. Everyone was crazy about her, so they couldn't stay mad at me. She just radiated joy and kindness.

One day when she was in the fourth grade, I got a phone call from her teacher who said Eseta had used a bad word on the playground. We were both surprised, because it didn't seem to be in her character. I asked the teacher how she usually handled such behavior with other children. She said she always put them in time-out. So I told her to treat Eseta the same as all of the other children. Sure enough, it happened again, and again Eseta was put in time-out by her teacher.

A few days later I was practicing the alphabet and early spelling with Eseta. I'd ask her to name three things that began with the letter "A," then "B," and so on. When we came to the letter "F," I again asked her to name three things that started with the letter "F." Eseta immediately said, "Frog." Then she gasped and clapped her hand over her mouth and said, "Oh, bad!" Well, that cleared up the question of using bad language on the playground. I think some of the boys were trying to get her in trouble and accused her of using "the 'F' word."

Eseta and Ray were very, very close. Her face lit up the minute he walked in the room. They just had a special bond. For some reason when she was about fourteen-years-old, she began to say, "Here comes my kind and generous father!" I have no idea where she picked up those words, but I'll tell you that sentence got her anything she wanted. Ray just melted.

We had Eseta Joy in our lives far longer than any of her doctors predicted. She was fifteen and a half when she and I spoke at a luncheon for The Adoption Exchange. She didn't seem to be feeling well that day. Two days later she developed strep throat. The infection went to her heart and she was hospitalized. Though she had great trouble breathing, there was nothing that could be done for her. We knew when we brought her home on Christmas Eve that we didn't have much time left with her.

We had our usual family holiday. I have a rule that the kids are not allowed to spend money on gifts. Each one has to give a gift that he made. It can be a poem or a song, or something crafted by hand. Each gift expresses love. And that is the sort of holiday we like. We had a great Christmas togther. That night Eseta asked if she could sleep in my bed, which was an unusual request. So I washed her, put fresh pajamas on her, and crawled into bed with her. She said her prayers, and waited for her dad to come into the room to kiss her goodnight. Several hours later, Eseta Joy died in my arms.

Eseta's birth mother came to her funeral and she was welcome to be there. Teachers and doctors and lots of friends were there too. I didn't want to lose her, but I began to visualize her dancing all over heaven and that helped me. Ray, on the other hand, was inconsolable. He never quit grieving for her. He wanted to be with her. He withdrew from other relationships and had a far away look in his eyes all of the time. I still see her in my mind and hear her voice. I am able to remember the joyful times, but Ray just couldn't get over the loss of his only daughter.

About a year ago I lost Ray too. I really think he just gave up on living after Eseta died. My consolation is the idea that when Ray died, Eseta was there to welcome him on the other side with the words, "Here comes my kind and generous father."

I still care for two adults who are severely disabled. A person could just sit around and feel sorry for herself. But that doesn't help. Sometimes it's really, really hard for me. But I'm doing what I love to do. I have four sons. They've turned out to be such fine adults. They learned a lot from Eseta. My sons include a teacher, an attorney and a doctor. But you know, Eseta was my greatest joy. She blessed us. She still does.

I'm the Blessed One

By Dixie van de Flier Davis, Ed.D.

Helen's husband died, leaving his wife and family of fourteen children on their Wyoming ranch. There had been plenty of love to go around in that family, so after giving birth to two children, Helen and her husband adopted twelve, always seeking out the children who needed them most.

That same afternoon a social worker called. Not knowing that Helen's husband had died only hours before, the social worker began to talk about a baby boy in a hospital seventy miles away who came into this life with only a brain stem. "He will always be deaf and blind and will never recognize people in his life," she'd told Helen. "But he needs a family."

There was an awkward moment when Helen said she was in the midst of planning her husband's funeral. But the conversation continued and before she knew it Helen had agreed to adopt Levi. That was eight years ago. Today Levi responds to the sound of his name and takes pleasure in his regular physical therapy exercises, often laughing out loud. Helen is convinced he may have some vision and she will see to it that he gets the best treatment.

There are twenty-one children in all who make up the Martin family - so far. Helen's three grown daughters help with the younger ones. And when the call comes in about another child, the four of them talk it over and almost always say yes. The family includes Sheila, who at the age of three was diagnosed with muscle mitrophy. Today she walks, climbs stairs and eats food from the table.

Helen said, "I am the blessed one. Each of the children brings me so much joy."

One of the most recent additions to the family is Christian, whose social worker asked Helen to fly 2,000 miles to meet this three-year-old "because he is ugly and I want you to see him before you make a decision."

Helen was immediately offended by this notion and refused to go. She told the worker, "We don't adopt a child because of how he looks. We adopt a child because he needs us." So Christian's foster parents drove him to Helen's home. Christian is six-years-old now and his adoptive family sees the beauty beneath his deformities. When Helen talks about Christian, she says "I am the blessed one, you know."

There is often a moment of hesitation when parents of deceased children are asked how many children they have. Do they want to open the wound and tell their story? But the lost child remains a part of the family. And so it is with Helen. Cody had cerebral palsy, a condition that left him vulnerable to infection. He died in his sleep at the age of nineteen, living much longer than his physicians ever predicted.

Thirteen years in the Martin family brought Jessica lots of hugs, laughter, and good times. Home is the best place to be when you're vulnerable or not feeling well. There is no substitute for loving hands of your own mother when the pain comes. At last Jessica died, leaving behind her memories of sweetness and family members who cherished their time with her. Again Helen reminded me that "I am the blessed one."

I begin to glimpse what she is saying. Helen is courageous enough to risk losing. She is open enough to allow herself to love and be loved without conditions. She is lucky enough to see below the surface of the skin and let her heart be transformed by the simple beauty of a child's soul.

Two years ago another call came. This baby boy too was born with microcephalis. He too needed a family.

"We named him Noah," Helen said. Noah didn't survive to come home from the hospital even once. He didn't live long enough for the system to execute court proceedings for a legal adoption. "But we claim him," Helen said firmly. One more life, despite how brief, has touched her. Once again Helen said yes to the opportunity to discover the depths of the love she is capable of giving and receiving. Helen claimed Noah and one more opportunity to let a child enter her heart. By now I wasn't surprised when she said, "Don't forget, I'm the blessed one."

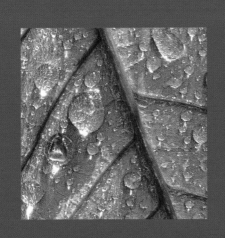

Desiree; Avery; and Kelsey

Lessons in Courage

About the time we started The Adoption Exchange I attended a workshop that left a big impression on me. One of the participants asked the speaker for some tips on running an event with no staff and no budget. The speaker began his answer with the words, "You can't do that." I looked around the room at the dedicated miracle workers from across the country and knew he'd said those words to the wrong group. Several courageous participants wiggled a bit in their seats and then said, "But we are!"

How is it that people are able to achieve the impossible?

Parents of disabled children work miracles every day. Again and again volunteers do what can't be done. Parents with HIV/AIDS face the impossible heartbreak of arranging for someone else to raise their children. I've come to the conclusion that there are seven essentials to accomplish what seem to be insurmountable tasks. These are some of the lessons.

♥ *Believe in yourself.* Even in the presence of some awesome talent, we have no reason to question ourselves. On the contrary, each of us complements the talents and skills of the other. In 1995 Joanne taught us this lesson. She asked us to help her find a family for her two sons because she was

HIV positive. They'd already lost their father to AIDS and Joanne faced the challenge of planning to let go of her children. We had no such program in place. But it was impossible to say no. In the years that followed, The Adoption Exchange helped families set up stand-by legal guardianship arrangements. We helped create memory books, photographs and video tapes to preserve their family stories. We gave families opportunities to learn from one another and support each other socially, with the goal of keeping these at-risk children from entering the foster care system.

♥ *Believe in the goal.* Research teaches us that when we are clear about the mission and hold that vision, our organizations grow to achieve it. A set of experiments known as the Pygmalion studies, carried out in classrooms with school children, demonstrated the power of another person's image of us in shaping our own performance. Teachers were told that one group of students was not very intelligent, tended to do poorly and was often not well-behaved, while the second group was bright, hard-working and successful. The teachers believed these to be the facts, though the division of the students into those two groups was actually random. Within one semester, with few exceptions, the children who were labeled as poor students were performing poorly and those labeled as good students were excelling. Whitney

and Trosten-Bloom, state that "if you want to transform a situation, a relationship, an organization, or a community, focusing on strengths is much more effective than focusing on problems."

For The Adoption Exchange, just as for adoptive families, it is important to remember the goal, the purpose. It is important for us to expect the best possible outcomes. Staying focused on the mission brings out the best in us and encourages us to support the best from others. Visitors to our offices often stop to look at the pictures of the children that cover our walls. Those children are our mission. The voices of the children are incorporated into every business meeting of our Board of Directors. With their future in our sights, we simply *have* to succeed.

♥ *Be eager to learn.* We get stale when nothing new is going on. There isn't a person alive who can't teach us something. We all learn from each other. The children we serve teach the most. Aristotle said, "A vivid imagination compels the whole body to obey it." And so it is in our world. When the people involved are learning, our creative energy makes things happen. We need to be asking ourselves again and again how we can do more, do it better, and find ways to do it faster - for the children. The creation of a permanency plan and choosing a caregiver for a child is undoubtedly one of the most painful tasks an HIV-infected parent has to face. But the future is somewhat easier for the children if the parents share what will happen when their family changes.

♥ *Believe in others.* We don't accomplish the impossible by ourselves. All kinds of people who lend support in big and small amounts are required. There is a place for everyone. Attorneys help set up stand-by guardianship papers. Women provide materials and set up scrapbooking groups on a Saturday morning. Employees in a corporate office purchase holiday gifts for children who might otherwise have none. Encouraged to do what they do best, ordinary people make miracles happen.

♥ *Take reasonable risks.* Probably half of what miracle workers get done is carefully planned. The other half is by "the seat of the pants." Since it isn't popular to say, "it just seemed like the thing to do at the time," we use words like innovation and entrepreneurial. But the truth is, we haven't always known exactly how we were going to get where we are going. Doing what can't be done means that people stay open to surprises and unexpected opportunities. The Adoption Exchange didn't have any funds to support a new program, but once we opened our eyes to the need Joanne brought to our attention, we began to identify ways to support the service. The money has followed.

♥ *Face challenges.* Sometimes you just have to get out there and lead. People and circumstances may contrive to throw up barriers. Sometimes negativism crowds its way into our thinking and our time. When that happens, doing the impossible has been a little more difficult. We've heard our share of well-intended, discouraging advice. A week before going on-air with our first televised fundraising and public awareness campaign, we were told that another organization had just raised a lot of money and there might not be any left. They were wrong. We've been told that someone who is pregnant can't love an adopted child, so it is better to let that child continue to grow up without parents. That wasn't accurate. We hear that people don't volunteer anymore and that teenagers won't let themselves be adopted. But we know that those who do the impossible face their challenges, make decisions that need to be made, and get the challenge out of the way. We put Joanne in a consultative role to help us design a program her committee called *Families Connecting For Kids*. Volunteers have stepped forward to create one-of-a-kind opportunities for these HIV/AIDS affected families. Only two of the children in these families have needed to access the foster care system.

♥ *Constantly reinvent.* The literature tells us that successful organizations continuously reinvent themselves and their programs. Successful people do the same, and Joanne's request is an example. She asked The Adoption Exchange to reinvent itself, just as she was so courageously working to reinvent her little family. The Adoption Exchange has changed as adoptive families asked for added services, and the adoption service community identifies new programs and training needs. Over time we watched Joanne lose weight and eventually her sons lost their mother. It was hard for all of us to face that loss, but hardest of all for those boys. The oldest was an angry teenager. We wondered if he would attend the memorial service. Joanne's smiling photograph stood at the front of the small church where she had found support in her last years. It broke our hearts to see seven-year-old Andy as he sat quite alone in the first pew. He stepped out and without any obvious cue was kneeling before his mother's photograph, when his older brother walked into the church, down the aisle and knelt beside him. When they quietly returned to their seats, a family who'd been standing by silently slipped in and wrapped their arms around them, ready to be the family to help them face the future. The last balloon in the big bouquet that was released after the service had this word written on it: Mommy. Birth parents and adoptive moms and dads reinvent themselves, refusing to give up hope in their children. Whether the challenges come from the parents' own physical illnesses, or due to the physical or emotional needs of their children, our staff have witnessed uncommon courage. We have responded as birth parents and adoptive parents have asked us to reinvent some of our services. And we have watched as mothers and dads allow love to redefine their families.

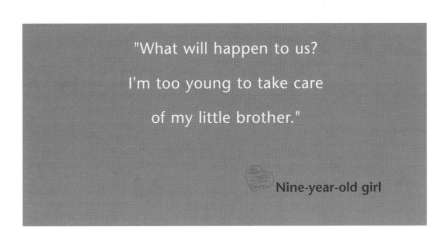

"What will happen to us?
I'm too young to take care
of my little brother."

Nine-year-old girl

Hope for Her Children

First published in *Heartlines* September 1995

One of the families taking advantage of the *Families Connecting for Kids* project is Luann, a warm and affectionate woman, and her children, six-year-old Mai, and two-year-old Anthony. These two children are very special to Luann, who faces a shortened life because of HIV and AIDS. She would like to start building a relationship with a family who could care for her children when she is no longer able to. Luann is in good health now, and is taking advantage of the time she has to spend with Mai and Anthony. The reality is that she isn't likely to live to see the children grow up. Nevertheless, she has dreams for her children and definite ideas about the kind of people she wants as Mai and Anthony's future parents.

Mai is a bright, sensitive little girl who likes to ride her bike, loves playing with her hamster Benny, and is eager to start dancing class. Anthony is an active, healthy little boy with a streak of stubbornness you'd expect of a child his age. He loves to be cuddled, likes to play ball, and do just about anything with Mai. The two children have a very close relationship.

When asked about what kind of people she would like to become future parents for her kids, Luann said she wants her children to be part of an affectionate family and to be guided by people who are open-minded and tolerant of people's differences. The children will need parents with whom they can freely share their grief and who will talk openly about their mom and dad as well as the reasons why they can no longer be together. Luann said it would be good for the children to have brothers and sisters and parents who had experience with children. Having been adopted herself, Luann is particularly sensitive to the importance of family relationships and wants her children to be accepted and loved as much as the family's birth children.

This is a unique and challenging situation for Luann and the family they hope to begin getting to know. Luann wants and needs all the time together as a family they can possibly have. For the resource family, there is the need for extraordinary patience and understanding. It is possible that Mai and Anthony will be able to live with their mom for many years. However, when the time comes that Luann can't parent on a regular basis, she wants to know that there is someone she knows and trusts to help out and take on the parenting role gradually. She also wants the children to come to feel that these new "friends" are like family. Luann wants a family that shares her basic values and hopes and dreams for the children so that she knows she is leaving her very special children in good care whenever the need arises. We wish Luann well as she makes every effort to enjoy and make plans for her children.

Life's Journey

By Arta Banks

In 1993 I decided to adopt a fifth child - a newborn baby. Before this, the youngest child I had ever adopted was eight-months-old. I had missed the bonding time that came with nighttime feedings, the first tooth, and other milestones like sitting up, crawling, and introducing solid food. The kids and I were so excited about the possibility of having a baby in our home and watching that child grow up.

Before I had completed my adoption paperwork, I found out about a little girl, not yet born but in need of a family. We were ecstatic. As we anxiously waited for her arrival, I had dreams about her. But nothing prepared me for the day I laid eyes on her. She was the most beautiful baby I had ever seen. Was she really going to be mine?!?!

It did not take long for the kids and me to fall in love with the baby girl we named Karmen. She quickly became queen of our household and it was not uncommon to find her siblings fighting over who would hold or feed her.

When Karmen was two-months-old, our excitement turned to grief. She was diagnosed HIV-positive with a life expectancy of only two years. I went into a three-day depression. Everything was normal by day, but at night I cried myself to sleep - if I could sleep.

I did not want my little girl to die. Parents aren't supposed to bury their children! I thought about all I would never see, including her high school graduation and her wedding day.

On the morning of the fourth day, I woke up and decided that I could spend her short life feeling sorry for myself or I could enjoy the time we had together. Scriptures I had memorized as a child began to flood my mind. They provided strength and encouragement. I had the voice of my father, who always told me that I am a Banks and that a Banks can do anything. I believed his words then and I needed to believe them now. I thought of my mother and how strong and courageous she was, and that gave me hope.

I decided that anything we had to do for Karmen would be normal. If we had to go to the doctor five times a day, it would be "normal" and we would adjust. I decided that if I wanted to see her in a wedding gown, I would make her one. I realized that although we may not see her graduate from high school, we could still celebrate every accomplishment in her young life.

With these thoughts in my mind, we began our journey. The road has been rocky at times, but we continue to celebrate her life. We go tent camping with medical supplies in tow. We push her in her wheelchair as we hike along rocky paths. We cry at times, but often we laugh.

Sometimes, when Karmen is really sick, I get sad and feel lonely. One night when I was feeling this way, I began having a pity party. Instead of my usual "can-do" attitude, I was thinking of how tough my life was. I looked up to the sky and said, "God, I know you said you would never give me more than I could handle, but I think you have me mixed up with somebody else." I instantly felt better. It was as if a huge load had been lifted from my shoulders. I had allowed myself to verbalize my humanness and it was a relief not to be super mom at that moment.

This journey we are on is not the one I chose when I decided that I wanted to adopt a baby, but it is the one I received when I fell in love with Karmen. I didn't have a choice about the fact that she is HIV-positive, but I am given a choice every moment to decide how I will respond to that fact.

Many times in life, we find ourselves in situations that are not what we wanted or anticipated. We must choose our response. We can sit around feeling sorry for ourselves, or we can face our challenges head on and make the best of them.

What will your choice be?

Arta Banks is a single mother of six children, five of whom are adopted. She is a published author of Wrong Feet First *and* Recipes and Remedies.

Banging on the Doors of Heaven

By Paula Pickle

When Serena was one-year-old, she and her brother were taken from her birth mother and put into a foster home. Then into another, and another, and another.

Over the course of three years, the two children lived in ten different foster homes. Abused and neglected by their birth mother, as well as several of their foster parents, their behavioral issues grew worse. Serena was violent, her brother defiant. Given their history they could easily have spent the rest of their childhood bouncing from foster home to foster home until they finally aged out of the system. But they didn't.

When Serena was four and her brother was seven, they were taken in by a foster family that wanted to adopt them. The wife was a social worker and knew both children needed special care. She took them to a program at a nearby children's hospital, where she was told by one doctor that Serena was too emotionally scarred to ever function normally in a family. "There is nothing we can do to help her," he informed her.

"I am not going to give up on a five-year-old child," was her immediate response.

And she didn't. Soon afterwards, the family relocated to Colorado, where there was a program designed for abused children like Serena and her brother. There the two children found the healing they needed.

Years later, on the day of Serena's confirmation, Serena saw her mother crying. When Serena asked her why, her mother said, "When you were little I banged on the doors of heaven, and God told me one day he would bring good out of all of this. Now I get to see that well."

Today Serena teaches in a Catholic school in Delaware. Her brother is married and has two children of his own. Looking back on how God brought them and her parents together, Serena says, "Some people don't want to take on other people's problems. But God is gracious and if he wants you to do something, he'll give you the graces you need to get through."

"There are lots of kids out there like my brother and me," she adds. "They're the ones often overlooked. But if people could just recognize that you never know what God is going to do and take a chance on those kids, so much good could be brought out of their suffering like it was with ours."

What Will Happen?

By Dixie van de Flier Davis

Julie and Robert have four children who have witnessed the horrors that HIV/AIDS can bring to a once content and active family. Robert is currently unable to get out of bed during the day and cannot do the things that once brought him joy like bathing his three-year-old son, Sam, or reading his daughter her favorite bedtime story. It takes all of Julie's energy just to get dinner made and the laundry done before she needs to take the eighteen pills that help keep her alive.

Their four children were terrified of what would happen to them if their mom and dad died. They began acting out in school, getting into fights, and became more withdrawn from each other during a time when they needed each other most.

Julie became involved with *Families Connecting for Kids* and received assistance getting her children therapy, school tutors, and education about HIV which has calmed some of their fears. Julie and Robert have established a legal plan for their pastor to become the children's guardian and they have learned to talk with their children about this plan to relieve their worries. Without the help of *Families Connecting for Kids*, these children may have continued on a downward spiral, fearful to communicate about their worries, and acting out their fears through violence at school.

Choosing a future caregiver for a child is undoubtedly one of the most painful tasks that an HIV-infected parent will have to face. Before Connie died, she had received help from *Families Connecting for Kids* to determine who would be the best caretaker for her two young children. She eventually asked her brother to become their future guardian. With the help of the program's volunteer attorneys, the children's uncle now has legal guardianship. They don't have to wonder who will take care of them. While they still have to deal with the loss of their mother, they can plan for their futures, including joining the basketball team, taking a ballet class, and learning to ride a horse. The children can concentrate on grieving the loss of their mother, while focusing on school and being kids, rather than worrying about where they will go.

"Adopting is VERY important to me because of the life that I grew up in. I am not the only kid that should get adopted. There are LOTS of other kids that should be adopted."

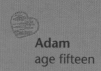

Adam
age fifteen

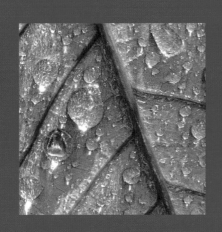

Chandranatha Family, Tom Mustin/CBS4, and Pat McDonnell/McDonnell Family Foundation; David; and Destiny

Getting More Than We Give

Parents teach lessons on courage and tenacity, determination and beauty. Twenty-five years ago I subscribed to the "Velveteen Rabbit" definition of beauty. I understood that when someone is loved-on for a long time, their ears begin to flop over, their eyes start to sag and their seams begin to fray. And that, I understood, was beautiful.

Today I have a different definition of beauty. I've learned that it is the one who does the loving that in the process becomes beautiful. The overweight dad with circles under his eyes from nights of sleep interrupted by the nightmares of his children is beautiful. The frazzled mother who hasn't time to set an elegant table because the trips to her children's doctors and therapists have taken her day is beautiful.

Lights in The Adoption Exchange offices burn late night after night. Staff members labor to organize recruitment activities, parent orientation meetings, educational seminars, adoption matching parties, and dozens of other things which help give permanent families to hundreds of children every year. Their clothes are wrinkled from long work hours. Lack of time and limited income may mean they haven't been shopping lately. For them it is not a job, it's a purpose. Each of them is beautiful.

Every year over 400 volunteers selflessly commit their best talents to give the children served by The Adoption Exchange a chance and a future. I look at the glowing face of the individual who continues to write a check for a monthly donation even when she is unemployed. I see the smiles of those who work long hours to prepare for an event and scarcely have time to comb their hair before the guests arrive. *They* are beautiful.

Each of our volunteers has different motivation. Some are adopted and want to ensure other children have the same chance at a forever family as they did. Others see a child on television and want to help in some way. Others know how blessed they are to have children of their own, but still want to reach out.

Jean is one of those volunteers. After retiring, she came into our Colorado office one day a week or more for at least eighteen years. That's 5,616 hours. She knew every one of the waiting children by name and exercised uncommon patience when families called with questions. Some weeks she would arrive unannounced to say, "I knew there would be more phone calls than usual when I saw the sibling group on *Wednesday's Child*. So I thought I'd better come in one extra day this week to help answer those phone calls."

Except for a few minutes of relaxation over lunch, Jean remained focused on her purpose scarcely putting the phone down.

Adoption parties were one of her favorite places to be. Waiting children come to these parties with their caseworkers hoping to have a good time and to meet someone who might eventually become their adoptive parents. Prospective parents come to get acquainted with children and to ask questions of the caseworkers and of experienced adoptive parents who are there with their children. There are games and plenty of food. Jean sat at the information table and gave each inquirer as much time as was needed. She knew the parents. She knew the children. And oh, how she loved the children.

A lot changed over the years. Jean adapted when we moved our offices. I asked if driving across town to the new location would prevent her from volunteering. She gently reminded me that she had carefully chosen where to volunteer. She came to our office each week because of the needs of the children, not because of the convenience of our location. So her commute simply became longer and she didn't complain. She came each week for five years after she began to require oxygen, pulling her tank behind her. And she didn't complain.

She didn't complain when one staff member left to attend graduate school or later when another moved out of state. Instead, Jean took a deep breath, ignored many chances to criticize, and graciously worked beside our disorganized and organized staff alike. Except for a coffee mug or expression of thanks, during those eighteen years Jean's only payback was knowledge of when a child had been adopted.

Jean receives our newsletters and gets an occasional phone call or greeting card from our staff even though her volunteering days are in the past. She watches the faces of the children on *Wednesday's Child* from the comfort of her home. And I hope she knows that we remember what she taught us. We remember the contributions she made to our lives and to the well being of the children we serve. Jean cared. She still cares. Jean possesses the beauty of a woman who knows how to love. How we miss her!

Colorado Springs volunteer, Bev, helped The Adoption Exchange because of the satisfaction that comes from seeing the kids get permanent homes. She shared information with the public weekly on KKTV Channel 11's feature *A Waiting Child* and provided emotional support to children waiting for adoption when they needed someone to confide in. We owe special thanks to the television stations in all our states that work tirelessly each week to assist in the mission of recruiting adoptive families for special children.

Elmer came into the office in July 2004 with a check in memory of his wife Constance. He explained that the children on *Wednesday's Child* broke her heart. She kept a jar on her dresser in which she would put her spare change for the children. When she passed away he felt he needed to honor her wishes and delivered a check for $340. He continues her tradition now and has a jar on his dresser. He has returned to the office with another check and a can of cookies.

Jeremy has been associated with The Adoption Exchange for ten years, six as a Board member. He became involved because he had been adopted. He helps with foster children, has donated his own funds, and gives freely of his time.

"Each and every day The Adoption Exchange works tirelessly to give children the gift of hope. Hope that there is a family waiting for them. Hope that will be realized once

they are united with a forever family. Each and every day, regardless of the season, The Adoption Exchange works to make sure that all the children waiting, hoping for a family, may someday have parents and homes to call their own," Jeremy said, "For as long as there is a child without a family, there will always be The Adoption Exchange. And for as long as there is The Adoption Exchange, I will continue to support this vital organization."

It is our donors and volunteers who help The Adoption Exchange stretch its resources and provide more services for children waiting to be adopted. Our success, like that of other non-profit organizations, depends upon lots and lots of people who set aside their own personal interests and offer what they do best to a cause that will change lives long after we are gone.

Every day since The Adoption Exchange opened its doors there have been lessons to learn. I often think I must have more to learn than most people and that's why I still enroll in the class every year. The children teach us about grief, survival, and coping. I have come to see that if they can let go of unspeakable hurts and shattering insults to their lives, we can learn to let go of petty annoyances and disappointments in our own. Working together gives the community the opportunity to heal our wounds and build something better for society.

In this chapter volunteers, board members, staff, and donors reveal how The Adoption Exchange touched their hearts and enriched their lives.

The Heart Aroused

Listen.

In every office

you hear the threads

of love and joy and fear and guilt,

the cries for celebration and reassurance,

and somehow you know that connecting those threads

is what you are supposed to do

and business takes care of itself.

By David Whyte

A Volunteer Who Truly Gives

First published in *Heartlines* Spring 1987

Bev gives her heart not only to children but to families as well. Every week, Bev shares information about the child featured on *A Waiting Child* on KKTV Channel 11 in Colorado Springs. Families interested in adoption receive their own dose of loving care from Bev as she tells them about the waiting child or about how to begin the adoption process.

Bev is uniquely qualified for this volunteer position. She and her husband are adoptive parents and she has helped provide classes in foster-adoption for El Paso County Social Services.

Why does she give so much time to help The Adoption Exchange? "The satisfaction comes from seeing the kids get a permanent home," says Bev. It really all began when she and her husband took their second child, Ryan, into their home through El Paso County's foster-adopt program. Because of the turmoil involved in waiting for his birth mother to relinquish him for adoption, "I made up my mind I was going to find out how this adoption stuff works." Bev sat through termination hearings in court and developed a real sensitivity to what birth parents go through in relinquishing a child.

Because of her own wish to have had a friend to talk to when she adopted her daughter, Kelli, as well as her son, she decided that she would be there when someone else needed a friend.

Several years ago, a teenage girl was filmed for *Wednesday's Child* in Albuquerque, New Mexico, and Bev was there. Bridgette, then fourteen, was quite scared, not only about the filming, but about being adopted. Bev took the crying girl for a walk and a warm talk. Bridgette was afraid that a family wouldn't like her. Bev, who saw a lovely and lovable young lady, helped calm her fears. Eventually, the reporter was able to walk quietly with Bridgette and the filming went well, resulting in an adoptive family for this young lady. Bev says that her experience of being able to help a child see the possibilities really made the difference.

The Gift of Hope

By Jeremy Flug

I have had the pleasure of being associated with The Adoption Exchange for ten years. I have also had the privilege of service on the Board for six of those years. I have been a member of various committees and chaired others. I have never hesitated to ask a potential donor to become a significant donor and have made The Adoption Exchange a priority as far as my own family's giving is concerned. All that said, I feel as though there is so much more that I could be doing given the number of kids without families.

Having been adopted myself, I make it a point each night to tell my four boys how lucky I am to have them in my life. To know that so many kids go to bed without this blessing is the reason why I am so committed to The Adoption Exchange, the reason why this organization is so important to me. Through the help of folks at The Adoption Exchange, I have been able to spend time with several foster kids who have a real tough time during the holiday season. These children lack the families and the love that many of us take for granted, the love that makes the holiday season so special for me and my family.

Sharing the holidays with these children has been a wonderful opportunity. It's an opportunity to offer encouragement, friendship, and even humor to those who need it most.

When I first met Tyler, a thirteen-year-old boy originally from Nebraska, it was clear to me how leery he had become of adults. During the two years prior to our introduction, he had been adopted, given back, adopted, and again given back to the foster care system. Because of these experiences, he was very afraid of becoming attached to someone for fear of ultimately being disappointed. He mentioned that he thought his caseworker had a family for him, but his voice let me know he wasn't going to keep his hope up.

Each and every day, The Adoption Exchange works tirelessly to give children like Tyler the gift of hope. Hope that there is a family waiting for them. Hope that will be realized when they are united with a forever family. Each and every day, regardless of the season, The Adoption Exchange works to make sure that all the children waiting, hoping for a family, may someday have parents and homes to call their own. For as long as there is a child without a family, there will always be The Adoption Exchange. And for as long as there is The Adoption Exchange, I will continue to support this vital organization. We are all very lucky to have them in our community.

"Twenty-five years ago I was looking for a worthy organization for my Girl Scout troop to volunteer for. Answering the first telethon phones with my young girls was the beginning of my volunteer service for The Adoption Exchange. Being part of an organization that to me has never faltered in its one true mission - to help children - has made me always proud to be one of their volunteers.
I was recognized in the past as one of the first volunteers. My comment, "it warms my heart to be a part of The Adoption Exchange."
it is truly what has guided me to remain as one of the volunteers all these twenty-five years."

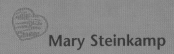

Mary Steinkamp

Joining the Cause

By Rick Brinnenman

'm not a 'joiner.' I have had a hard time involving myself with a non-profit organization beyond giving money. I've always thought, "Money is easy, but the time given is precious." I've learned better. It takes generous amounts of both for an organization to be successful.

My path to becoming part of The Adoption Exchange started when I was about three-years-old, in the early 1950s, when my birth father relinquished me for adoption. My adoptive parents, Jean and Buck, found me. Through their wonderful love and caring, I became part of a family that has supported me throughout my life.

Fast-forward thirty years. I was working as a photographer at KOAT, an Albuquerque television station that aired *Wednesday's Child*. The children, much like I had been, were searching for families. At the time, I always hoped they would find what they were searching for and felt if I took the right picture maybe it would help connect a child with a family. Maybe the right angle would capture that heart.

Fast-forward another fifteen years. The Adoption Exchange was on the brink of leaving New Mexico because of financial constraints. The CEO of the company I was working with asked if I would be an advisor to the group to help keep The Adoption Exchange in

New Mexico. I said yes and joined the Advisory Group. He generously committed enough funds to keep the organization afloat and the doors of the New Mexico Office unlocked.

I have been with the organization ever since in whatever capacity they'll have me. My main goal is to find and connect people with The Adoption Exchange who understand that every child deserves to have a family and to expand the reach of the Advisory Group. My business side understands the need to translate funds into numbers of adoptions. My life experience tells me that a child being gathered into the arms of a loving, caring family has a value far beyond the dollars and far beyond the time given to the search. It is a joining I've found that I can be part of. It is an organization to which I want to give more than just money; I want to give my heart.

"Being a volunteer with The Adoption Exchange keeps me grounded. When I hear the children's stories and see their pictures in the picturebook and on the website, I want to take each and every one of them home and give them the permanent loving family that they deserve. Being a volunteer with The Adoption Exchange gives me the opportunity to help all the children find that permanent home."

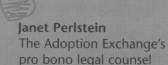

Janet Perlstein
The Adoption Exchange's
pro bono legal counsel
for fifteen years

"We have adopted three children from the foster care system

and are loving every minute we are having with them in our lives.

You do a great job caring for these kids and helping them,

keep up the good work! All children should find a good

and loving home to call their own forever and ever."

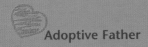

Adoptive Father

Understanding the Need

By Pam Kiker, *Board Chair 2004-Present*

In my business, I am blessed with the opportunity to work with families as they consider the purchase of a new house. It doesn't matter whether the house is $200,000 or $2,000,000, whether it has laminate countertops or granite, whether it is 1,200 square feet or 12,000 square feet – until the family moves into the house it is only a house. Then it becomes a home. The first-time buyers that we work with typically own their homes from three to five years and then they move up. Our experienced buyers usually have their homes from five to ten years. There they watch their families grow up and go out on their own, and the empty nesters finally choose to downsize their homes to fit their new lifestyles. All of these families choose when to move. They have the option to provide a new home for their families. Their permanence in any home is by their choice, by their selection.

The challenge of The Adoption Exchange is an extremely heart-breaking one. It is the challenge of helping find homes for the children, not just houses; and providing guidance, support, and education for the families of these children so that their placement will be a "forever home".

Let me take just a few minutes to refresh your memories about the life of one of The Adoption Exchange's and one of my friends, David.

David was born in June 1973. When David was a baby, he was adopted and almost immediately put back into foster care as his adoptive parents were older and not able to deal with David's disabilities. David has cerebral palsy and is confined to a wheel chair.

When he was several years older, David was adopted by another family and then put back into foster care when his parents divorced. His parents kept their biological children and returned their adopted children to foster care. David was six years old.

In June 1985 The Adoption Exchange met David. He was a *Wednesday's Child* on several occasions, but was never adopted again. The biography of David when he was twelve-years-old that was given to potential adoptive parents contained these words: "David loves chasing games and physical contact, especially tickling. He gets along well with his teachers and classmates in a classroom for developmentally disabled children. He likes math best and reading least since his reading skills are somewhat delayed. David's social worker is looking for a couple or single parent for him. He would like to maintain contact with his two brothers."

When David was fifteen his biography contained this information: "This personable young man has discovered the computer and uses it to write and to play chess and checkers. He is enrolled in junior high where he gets A's in most of his classes. In reading and math he is at third grade level and is making excellent progress.

David is very personable and has many friends. He is determined to do as much active living as possible from his wheelchair. He currently enjoys playing basketball, shooting a bow and arrow, and bowling. David really wants a parent or parents of his own - someone who can understand his challenges and help him prepare for an independent adult lifestyle. All families will be considered."

In 1989 when David was almost sixteen-years-old, The Adoption Exchange writes: "David is a personable young man and delightful to have around. Like most fifteen-year-olds he likes pizza and spaghetti, although he will eat just about anything. He enjoys typical teenage activities including going to movies and malls. He can pretty much take care of himself, but needs assistance with getting into or out of his wheelchair, into his shower chair, or the car. He is able to do a lot of chores including bringing his own laundry to the laundry room, putting his clean clothes away, and vacuuming the basement weekly. Like most youngsters, he'd be happier if chores weren't required, but he is cooperative about doing them. David says that he would like a two-parent family with brothers and sisters."

In 2004 David is old enough to be on his own. He lives by himself in an apartment in Denver, is a teacher's aide to elementary school children and helps them with their math. He has taken several driving lessons, is quite independent, capable of shopping for himself, caring for his two cats, and cooking his own meals; though he definitely would rather eat Italian food out! David is now thirty-one-years-old.

David and I often talk about the Post Adoption Services Program we are working to develop. David is willing to support The Adoption Exchange in any manner that he can to help this program be a success. He would love to counsel the full time staff member that will work on this program. You see, he would do anything to make sure that other children don't have to go through what he has had to endure. David still does not have a "forever family".

The Adoption Exchange received a grant from the state of Colorado to provide post-adoption services for families adopting out of the system in communities throughout the state. We are working to ensure that services like these will continue and expand to serve adopted children across the country, no matter how they were adopted. The stories of young men like David will become fewer and fewer. His story will be the exception rather than a story frequently heard. David's life is very much a story of success as to what he has accomplished on his own, but equally as much a story of how the system has failed.

Our support will mean long-term opportunities for children not to go from house to house, but to have what they so dearly want - a permanent home of their own.

"The Adoption Exchange has become a mature and highly respected organization in the adoption community. I can remember when it was a fledgling not-for-profit and we were assembling its first board of directors. I am so very proud of how far the organization has come over the past twenty years and the many children and families it has served. Congratulations to a terrific and dedicated staff."

Elaine Gantz Berman, First Board Chair
1983-1986

"Ask yourself 'What does caring mean?' I think of the many dedicated and caring volunteers, employees, companies, patrons, and board members that are the heart behind the Heart of The Adoption Exchange. Ask yourself 'What does caring do?' I think of making a loving child smile a thousand times over. I think of The Adoption Exchange and for it I am thankful."

Rich Montoni, Board Chair 1986-1990

"I became involved with The Exchange because I was impressed with the cause of finding permanent loving homes for all kids. I was especially impressed with the efforts to keep sibling groups together as they are adopted. I have been rewarded over my twenty plus years with The Exchange by being able to say that I have been able to help in finding homes for over 4,600 kids."

Don Butt, Board Chair 1990-1994

"The Adoption Exchange is an organization that is dedicated to the single mission of endeavoring to find a 'forever, loving home' for every child who needs one. This mission is approached in a totally unbiased manner with regard to race, ethnicity, religion, sexual orientation, or gender; while each of these factors is taken into careful consideration. In this process, the organization has developed an intolerance to the word 'no.' One of the underlying cornerstones of the organization is 'there is always a way.'"

Larry Walker, Board Chair 1994-1997

"Every time I heard Dixie tell a story about a child who was waiting, I realized that I could never think of not being involved with The Adoption Exchange."

Robert Griffith, Board Chair 1997-2000

"Children who are enriched with a forever family really feel what it means to trust, to care, to love, and to be loved. I can think of no greater reward for those of us involved with The Adoption Exchange than to help make that dream of a permanent family a reality for so many children."

David Zinger, Board Chair 2000-2004

The Organ

By Shelbi Perry

A few weeks ago, I was notified that May Dee Fields wanted to donate her Hammond organ to an adoptive family who could use it. I contacted Mrs. Fields and she told me that her husband was in a nursing home and she wanted to get rid of some things in the house that are no longer of use to her. COPARC (Colorado Post-Adoption Resource Center) got the word out to its families and we collected names of those who were interested. We drew the winning family's name. It was the Chandranatha family of five children; three adopted and two whose adoptions are almost final.

Later, Mrs. Fields called me and thanked us profusely for the experience. When the Chandranatha's came to pick up the organ, she said one of the little girls sat down in front of the organ and "made it sing". The family invited her over to their house and she accepted. All five of the children performed on the organ and gave her a little "concert". As they began to get to know each other, they realized that they had a lot in common. They had both lived in Texas and had family members that attended the same college in Alabama. Mrs. Fields said that there was more love in that family than she had witnessed in a long time. They will continue their friendship and it seems as though this family will become somewhat of an "adoptive" family for a sweet, elderly woman who might get lonely from time to time. A wonderful connection was made and it brings tears to my eyes!"

Grace's Story

By Barbara Mattison, M.A., was Director of Programs when The Adoption Exchange was founded in 1983.

We first saw Grace on *Wednesday's Child* 10 years old, functioning just above the developmentally disabled range and needing a family. Grace's birth mother, a drug addict and a prostitute, had left her in her grandmother's care, but grandmother was unable to care for Grace's diabetes or to keep her away from sexually abusive relatives. Grace had been gang raped repeatedly by her uncles and burned with cigarettes by her aunt. Grandmother's rights were terminated when Grace was 7; by age 10, Grace had had eleven crisis care and foster care moves.

When I first saw Grace, her soft brown eyes melted me and I knew we were her family. Grace came home to our two-parent, three-kid household and we had a good month before the acting out started. This poor kid - so angry, so scared, so needing control and so unattached - did everything in her power to protest being part of our family. She had screaming tantrums, she cut the phone cords, she acted out sexually, she overdosed on insulin, she convinced classmates to buy her candy, and she thrust a lead pencil deep into a classmate's leg. After Grace's third brush with death through self-induced diabetic coma, we told Grace's therapist and Children's Hospital that we were exhausted and that we didn't feel we could keep her safe.

Grace spent six months in the Children's Hospital psychiatric unit and was discharged to a residential treatment facility, the youngest girl they had ever taken. Grace wanted to come home - we said we couldn't do it and life got very emotional for all of us as we worked on how to parent Grace at a distance. We worked out regular activities - just with the two of us as parents - two to three times a month.

A stint in jail for assault and battery after discharge from residential care was a huge eye-opener for Grace - she wanted no part of jail, but it did lead to her connection with Louise, a woman taking care of her incarcerated sister's children. Louise took Grace under her wing and they all moved to Los Angeles. We began a regular long distance relationship by phone. The relationship with Louise grew strained; Louise decided to move to Kansas, and Grace met a young man named Larry. We went to California, met Larry, and helped them get into an apartment. Grace enrolled in a GED program, and actually graduated from high school - the first person in her family ever to achieve that.

Grace's relationship with Larry, although frequently rocky, has continued now for ten years. She and Larry have two children. They live with Larry's brother and several others in a house in Los Angeles. Grace has just started a barber training program. Even though life is not easy for her, she has achieved more success than any other member of her family. Grace is now 33 years old. We talk regularly - generally two to three times a month. We visited her and her family a few weeks ago and it was a great joy to be with her and Larry and their children. All of our lives have been, and are being, transformed.

Always in our Hearts

We've been away from the Rocky Mountains for sometime, but we as a family will always remember your *Wednesday's Child* program. It always touched our hearts. I've often wondered why a state as big as Illinois doesn't feature the same program. Every child deserves a loving home and it's a shame that nothing here is done as effective as your program.

I'm sure you heard of the two little girls here who were abandoned by their parents last Christmas. We as a family were so upset by this that we wrote offering to adopt the little girls. Every time I tucked my little girls in who were the same ages, I ached for those little girls.

We have seven wonderful children who are growing up into wonderful responsible children and adults. I know this is because of the love and support they found at "home."

Enclosed is twenty dollars. I wish we could do more, but we just wrote out tuition checks for two colleges!

If there is anything I can do to help, please let me know.

In the Moment

By Kelly Blair Roberts,
Administative Supervisor, 1983-1985

As an administrative assistant for the then Rocky Mountain Adoption Exchange in the 90s, I had the distinct honor of helping with the first telethon. As a thirty something, not married and not a parent, I wondered what in the world would compel these adoptive parents to adopt special needs children. I heard but didn't really understand their stories of how they got as much if not more than the kids they took into their lives.

Fast forward to the 2000s. As a 50 something, I home hospiced both my parents. What a profound impact this had on my life. I even went on to become a professional caregiver. And you know what? I got it. I got what the adoptive parents were talking about.

The role of adoptive parent is similar to the role of a caregiver because the gifts that come with these roles are similar. The gift of doing for others is of course rewarding. But the gift I most treasure as a caregiver is the exquisite opportunity to slow down and be in the moment with another human being. And the needs of children are not that different from the needs of frail elders.

The Adoption Exchange is a conduit—for special needs children to be matched with people who are receptive to the gifts that can only come from opening your heart.

A Gift to My Family

By Richard M. Hess, Jr.

I first joined the Board of Directors of The Adoption Exchange in 1993. Keeping track of my involvement has been easy as my son, Matt, was born in December of that year. My children have grown up with The Adoption Exchange as my involvement has always included the whole family. Matt and later Annie, who was born in 1998, have attended many events including board dinners, volunteer recognition parties, and adoption matching parties.

Given the profound needs of the waiting children and the heroism of the people who open their hearts and homes to them, I have often felt that my impact was insignificant.

In addition, I am well aware that any contribution that I have made has been dwarfed by what The Adoption Exchange has given to my family. Also, whenever we have made a contribution of any type or size, we have always felt appreciated. The Adoption Exchange knows how to say "thank you," and loves its volunteers.

I would like to share two examples of The Adoption Exchange's impact on our lives. The first occurred six or seven years ago at an informal board dinner. My whole family attended and Annie, age two at the time, provided entertainment in the form of standing on her head and showing off her underwear. Matt listened attentively to the stories of the waiting children that Dixie shared with us. After dinner he looked across the table at Joan Prugh, a fellow Board member and an adoption social worker by profession, and asked, "What's child abuse?" Joan was great as she sensitively tried to explain to Matt about the experiences of these children. The expression on Matt's seven-year-old face was striking. Clearly, he found it difficult to believe Joan as she spoke about how adults had betrayed the trust of so many children. As I thought about Matt's reaction it occurred to me that it is the right of every child to grow up with the inability to comprehend the idea of child abuse. The hope and prayer of my entire family is that maybe one day The Adoption Exchange will become obsolete.

When Matt was almost twelve we were attending another of these dinners and he heard me describe my involvement with The Adoption Exchange as a family project. I spoke of how Matt and Annie had grown up with The Adoption Exchange and related that Matt had attended his first telephone fund raiser when he was four-months-old. He spent that entire evening asleep in his car seat. On the drive home Matt asked me about what happened when I had volunteered to telephone donors. I described making the calls and explained that the pledges that are received are an important part of the preparation for each annual "A Day for *Wednesday's Child*" on Channel 4. Without a moment's hesitation Matt declared that he wanted to make calls with me that coming year.

Four months later as I was preparing for the board meeting preceding that year's scheduled telephoning of donors, I was thinking about how I might challenge fellow board members to sign up to make calls. Matt's willingness to volunteer came to mind. First, I checked with Matt to see if he still wanted to make calls, being very careful to give him a ready out just in case he had any second thoughts. There was not the slightest hesitation on his part and I was astonished by his enthusiasm. Later that same day, I was proud to use Matt as an example as I challenged the whole board to make a commitment to volunteer that year. After all, if a twelve-year-old boy was excited about volunteering, nothing should prevent these adults from doing likewise.

The evening to make calls arrived and we headed off to Navigant International's offices. As we ate pizza and went through orientation I realized that I had forgotten about the many steps that were involved in making each call. As volunteers contact donors they collect or confirm important information and complete pledge forms and other materials. It was apparent that the process would be tough for a twelve-year-old to manage by himself. Matt and I decided to work as a team. I would feed him the information and fill out forms while he made the calls. Being a protective Dad, I set him up for some initial success. I had Matt call his grandfather, godfather, other family members, and friends. Each of these people were touched by Matt's zeal and responded generously.

After a bit we called another close family member. As I listened to Matt's side of the conversation I could tell that this person was grilling him about The Adoption Exchange and its work. He did a great job and with the help of our "cheat sheet" answered all of the questions. I was a very proud Dad. Next Matt asked this person if he would consider making a pledge. Suddenly, Matt looked bewildered and mouthed to me that this person told him that they "never give to telephone solicitors!" Neither of us could believe it. We weren't strangers! Quickly I told Matt to ask whether we could send an information packet. He quickly did so and without missing a beat stated in a very firm and forthright manner, "I hope you will carefully consider supporting The Adoption Exchange because I believe that every child deserves to live in a permanent, loving home".

To this day I get emotional as I tell this story. No where in the script or other materials that we were using that night will you find these exact words. This statement came straight from my little boy's heart. Words cannot express how grateful I am to The Adoption Exchange for its role in the development of the sensitivity and strength of character that my son displayed that night. The Adoption Exchange has given my family so much more than we will ever be able to give in return.

The Early Days

By Mary Dreger, MSW,
Director of Community Resources 1983-1987

The little four room office of The Adoption Exchange on East Colfax seemed drab and tired when I first entered it in 1983 as a student from Metro to interview for an internship. The orange three-ring binder on the table that held about two dozen photos of children waiting for adoption was the only spot of color in the deserted waiting room. The hallway was dark and the offices were empty, except for the bright one at the end of the hallway where a cheerful voice invited me in and introduced herself as Dixie, the first director of this fledgling non-profit agency. Over tea I learned that child advocates and social workers, frustrated with the plight of thousands of children vegetating in foster care, had sought funding for a project that focused entirely on finding permanent, adoptive homes for special needs children across the Rocky Mountain Region. The Piton Foundation, spear-headed by Elaine Berman, responded with funding for a coordinated and cooperative effort. And now this agency was off the ground. Dixie didn't miss a beat and went off to open a checking account and along the way recruited the banker, Jack Bowles, as a contributor!

As Director of Community Resources, my role was to recruit volunteers and funders to help us in our mission to connect waiting children with loving families. And help they did!! Every day there was reason to be grateful for an act of love and generosity from someone in our community. Those families who gave the ultimate gift - a permanent place for a homeless child - filled our hearts. Others reached out in different ways generously giving of themselves in whatever way possible to grow and develop The Adoption Exchange.

I remember standing in front of the small television monitor at the first *Wednesday's Child* Docuthon held in the store front office of the Sentinel Newspaper. (It too was a fledgling effort with maybe twelve people on the phones). *Turn on Your Heart Light*, the theme from the movie *E.T.*, came on as the show opened and my eyes filled with tears of gratitude for the help and expertise of Lon Lee, Kerralyn Garma, Sharon Levy, Roger Ogden, and so many others at KCNC CBS4 who gave of their time and talents to make The Adoption Exchange successful. These highly visible fund-raising events along with *Wednesday's Child* weekly features were the cornerstone in our efforts to raise the issue of permanency planning for children, promote special needs adoption, and raise funds to sustain our efforts over the long-term. Volunteers enthusiastically organized every sort of special event fundraiser, contributing hours of time and effort because they cared, because they believed, and because they wanted to put their concern and their beliefs into action to make a difference for children. And they shared in the joy of connecting families with children.

The community contributed in so many ways in those early days. As I read the newsletter now I am heartened by the fact that so many of the early supporters are still actively involved. Epicurean Catering supported our first corporate luncheons and another anonymous donor presented a surprise donation at a telethon well over twenty years ago that took my breath away! These supporters are like the adoptive families who know that not only love, but continuing commitment is required. This continuing commitment will sustain The Adoption Exchange for another twenty-five years.

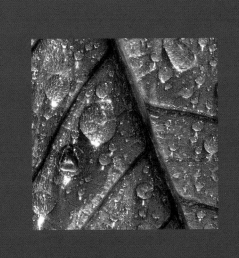

Ian; Jacky; Jeffery and Natasha

Don't Stop Trying for Me

I am told that the standard greeting among Masai warriors is *kesserian ingera*. Translated to English, this means, *"and how are the children?"* The greeting suggests that a high value is placed on the well-being of the children in the Masai society. Always the desired response is, *"All the children are well."* Whether the warrior is himself a parent or childless, the concern is that peace and safety prevail, that the priorities of protecting the young are in place. It means the community remembers its reason for being, its functions and responsibilities. Even when times are tough, it is a priority that the Masai children are cared for.

What would happen today if we began our greetings this way? What if we passed the question along ten or fifteen times a day and if we each felt an equal weight for the daily care and protection of the children?

What would our world be like if our President began every press conference by answering the question, *"Mr. President, how are the children?"*

On October 26, 2002, the Orphans' Monument was dedicated at Riverside Cemetery, the oldest cemetery in Denver, Colorado. For years twenty-two children from the old orphanage shared a common grave unmarked by a headstone. One visitor to the cemetery was so disturbed by this that she gave the caretaker a few dollars to start a fund to purchase a tombstone and his mission began.

One year later Cliff Dougal had raised the dollars he needed. He planned an appropriate graveside ceremony. Roz Brown, a local entertainer and folk singer, sang some songs that were relevant to the occasion. Twenty-two doves representing the children buried there were released. The people who attended included former residents of the orphanage, people who had grown up without parents and still struggled to find their place in the world. There were some adopted children who asked to attend and who brought flowers. Each had his own story to tell, if anyone stopped to listen. Some stayed to meditate next to the grave, never revealing the nature of their own pain.

Today the answer would have to be that thousands of our children are not safe and cared for. Like the twenty-two children who were recognized by the dedication of that headstone and who have gone unnoticed for many decades, there are 114,000 children in the USA today who are largely invisible. These children long for family, for a home, for someone to love, and for someone to love them. They wait for adoption after the trauma of abuse and serious neglect.

There are many ways to abandon a child.

If we do not take action today to give these thousands of waiting children safety and love with moms, dads, aunts, uncles, and grandparents, then we leave them faceless and alone. Cliff and all of the supporters helped create meaning in the lives and passing of those twenty-two. That place now gives testimony to their longings - to their unrealized hopes - their dreams cut short.

To James, Ed, Darrel, Freddie, Earl, and Georgia; to June, Oscar, George, Phillip, Hellen, Carrie, and Willie; to Joseph, Thomas, Louise, Maud, and Charlette — and to the child known only by the last name of Stephens - I say, "We have *not* forgotten you."

We say to the children, "This resting place and this monument give you a voice after all your years of silence. You remind us that if we are quiet and listen to our own hearts, we can hear the question, 'and how are the children?'"

We have a job yet to do to honor the lives of those whose futures were cut short. At The Adoption Exchange we're proud of twenty-five years of service to waiting children. But we are far from satisfied. We can't rest as long as there are children who wait for love, safety, and stability in families of their own.

Billy, twelve-years-old, is representative of the children who still wait for a forever family. In a letter to The Adoption Exchange, Billy writes:

"Hi, my name is Billy and I am looking for a loving, caring home. I want to tell you about myself. I love to play baseball (even though I'm not that great at batting). I also play basketball. I am looking for a home that does things together. A home that can be a permanent home a trusting home. I would like to be in a permanent home because I am tired of moving around all the time and I want to keep a loving relationship for the rest of my life. Being adopted is not just being with a family for the rest of my life it is feeling like I belong with that family the rest of my life. I want to not only have a relationship I want to have a strong one. This is why I not only want to be adopted I want to be accepted."

Kenni was adopted at age eleven after years of neglect that often found her without food or a warm home. She was left alone often and felt the only one who cared about her was her dog.

She said, "I now know that a Mother and a Father are not someone that gives birth to you - it is someone who loves you and takes care of you. My Mom and Dad love me very much. They have given me a nice, clean home to live in, they provide food for me to eat, and clean clothes to wear. They support me in everything I do."

"I hope that every child has the same opportunity to be adopted as I have had. There are too many children who are not being taken care of in the way that they deserve. My wish is for every child to be adopted into a loving home."

And this from a fourteen-year-old foster child, "God, if you're listening, I really want a family."

We long to proclaim, "The children are well." We work to say, "Yes, ALL the children are well."

In this chapter Mike, Kenni, Cherrie, Chris, David, and Joshua express the hope of all the children.

Alone

As I sit here with my thoughts
I wonder why
I will face the world alone
until I die.
My heart is full of sadness
Feeling sorry for myself
For I've no one to love me,
No, not even myself.
Everybody has someone,
Everybody has a home.
Nobody knows the feeling
Of what it's like to be alone.
Life seems to work
For everyone but me.
I'm loving someone,
But that someone doesn't love me.
I really wish I had a family
I really wish I had a home.
I really wish I had a someone,
So that I wouldn't be alone.

By Chris
age twelve

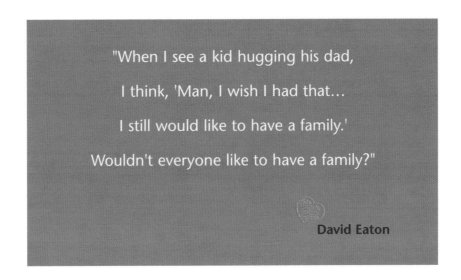

"When I see a kid hugging his dad,

I think, 'Man, I wish I had that...

I still would like to have a family.'

Wouldn't everyone like to have a family?"

David Eaton

Mike's Letter

I am writing to tell you about myself and my needs. I would like to have my hair hang over one of my eyes (preferably the right eye). I would like considerate parents that would spend time with the children and when gone would get a sitter.

I am twelve-years-old and am smart in my own eyes. I am kind of good on the computer. I also enjoy football, basketball, movies, and teasing my sisters. I believe in the LDS church, a good movie, being fair to your friends, and parents being appropriate with their children.

I like animals and I think I would feel comfortable in a family that had pets especially a German Shepherd (or a large reptile). You don't have to go buy one if you don't have one already.

I want to be adopted because being a foster kid is not the best. You have to move around all over the place and you don't feel like a "real kid." If I was adopted, I would feel like I was "real" like everybody else.

I Am a Foster Child

I am a foster child
I wonder if I'll always be
I hear people talk
I see nothing change
I want to be adopted
I am a foster child.

I pretend that I am not
I feel lonely
I touch my parents hand
To guide me through
I worry if my dreams will
Ever come true
I cry when I'm hurt
I am a foster child.

I understand I am
I say my feelings
I dream of having a family
I try to be patient
I hope to be adopted
I am a foster child.

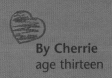

By Cherrie
age thirteen

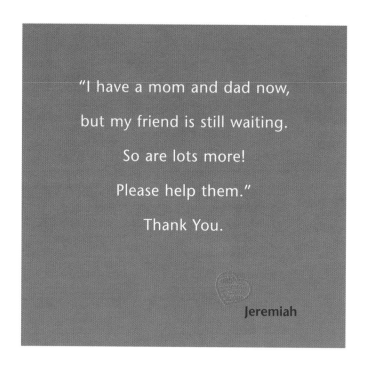

"I have a mom and dad now,

but my friend is still waiting.

So are lots more!

Please help them."

Thank You.

Jeremiah

Being a Foster Kid

I've lived with eight different families.

I've been a foster kid since 1996.

I have two sisters and seven brothers.

I do not know where they live.

When I was going to be a foster kid, a guy lied to me

when he said he would come back and get my stuff.

He didn't go get it.

I've lived in Kearns four times, Youth Services one time,

West Valley three times, and West Jordan one time.

Since I've been in foster care I've been to Idaho three times,

Colorado five times, Cedar City one time,

and Grand Junction two times.

By Joshua
age nine

"I hope that every child

has the same opportunity

to be adopted as I have been.

There are too many children

who are not being taken care of

in the way that they deserve.

My wish is for every child to be

adopted into a loving home,"

Kenni, age eleven,
adopted into her forever family
after being in foster care
for four and a half years.

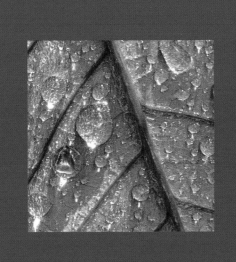

It's Time to Act

Currently, more than 114,000 children in the United States are waiting for adoptive parents to release them from the uncertain future of living in foster care. These children are in foster care because of traumatic abuse, neglect and abandonment. Many are considered "hard-to-place" because they are school-aged, members of sibling groups who don't want to be separated, are coping with physical disabilities, and struggling with emotional challenges as the result of their painful pasts. They are our nation's waiting children. And what they all want, more than anything, is a family to love them.

Tommy is only one of the 114,000 waiting children:

Thomas, who prefers to be called "Tommy", is a very intelligent and articulate fourteen-year-old who enjoys kickboxing and anything to do with cars. He is an avid

reader and he seems to genuinely enjoy participating in conversations on just about any topic. He just finished involvement in his local library's summer reading program. Tommy does well in the eighth grade and performs at grade level in all subjects. He is a wonderful young man and he will be a great addition to the right family! Like all children, Tommy needs nurturance, patience and stability to reach his full potential. To find out more about Tommy, make sure to inquire as soon as possible!

Don't make him wait! Tommy deserves a forever family of his own.

You can help by visiting The Adoption Exchange website, www.adoptex.org, or calling 1-800-451-5246 to learn more about children waiting for forever families and how you can become an adoptive parent. You can also help these children by volunteering or donating to The Adoption Exchange.

Steps to Adoption

Are you ready to learn more about adopting? The process varies from state to state. For more specific information please call The Adoption Exchange at 1-800-451-5246 or visit our web site www.adoptex.org. We can provide you with the name and telephone number of your state's Adoption Specialist.

Read. Books about adoption are available at your local libraries, bookstores, and The Adoption Exchange. Join an Adoptive Parents Group. Many adoptive parent groups welcome parents who are waiting to adopt. Other adoptive parents can answer many of your questions from first-hand experience.

Decide What Kind of Adoption You Want to Pursue. Your options include infant, waiting child, international, open, closed, private agency, and public agency. You will want to gather more information to help you decide what type of child you feel you can best parent.

Select an Agency. Interview agencies to find the right fit for you. We encourage you to attend orientation meetings offered by public and private agencies in your area. Although you must ultimately select one agency to work with, you are free to gather information from as many agencies as are available, even if you don't live in that agency's region. If you live in a rural area, you may have to make yourself available to travel to the nearest metropolitan area to get the adoption services you need.

Attend Orientation and Information Classes. Some public and private agencies require you to attend a series of classes to learn about the adoption process and emotional and behavioral issues that adopted children may experience. In many cases, you must complete these classes before the agency will begin the family assessment process.

Complete the Family Assessment Process. The family assessment (also called an adoption study or home study) is an educational and self-evaluation process as well as a way for the social worker to get to know you and your family and help you determine what child would best fit into your home. The family assessment includes some or all of the following: autobiographies written by each parent, a visit to your home, medical reports from your physician, proof of employment/ability to financially support a child, checks for any criminal record, (including the state child abuse registry), references from friends and associates, participation in adoptive parent training classes, a psychological evaluation, and a family picture book or video to present to the birth mother, waiting child, or overseas agency.

Child Search. Once your family assessment is completed, your social worker should be considering your family for a child/ren in that agency's custody. After being selected, you will be given extensive information about the child so that you can decide if this child is a good fit for your family. Some social workers, both with public and private agencies, may encourage you to be involved in the search for a child. Always let your social worker know what you are doing to help identify a child.

1. You may look at photo listing books of waiting children; watch for waiting child features in newspapers, adoption newsletters, and magazines; watch television features about waiting children. (e.g., "*Wednesday's Child*"); and access web sites on the Internet (e.g. www.adoptex.org).

2. You may register with regional or national adoption exchanges, which may assist you in your search.

Pre-placement. During this time you may visit with the birth family of the infant you plan to adopt, have several visits of increasing length with your child from foster care, or begin making travel plans to bring home the child you plan to adopt internationally.

Placement. Your child finally comes home!

Post-placement. Your agency, social worker, parent group, and professional counselors can help your family during this often challenging time. The social worker will be required to visit with you, provide support and assistance, and make reports to the court to be sure the placement is progressing well before finalizing the adoption. During this period, you will need to file a petition to adopt with the court.

Finalization. Your social worker or lawyer will usually go to court with you to make the child you are adopting a legal member of your family. Most infant adoptions are finalized six months after placement. Waiting child adoptions are usually finalized a year after placement in order to give the child and family sufficient time to adjust and be sure that the family can successfully meet the child's needs.

Post-Legal Period. We'll be here to support you. Adoption is a lifelong process for the child and the adoptive family. Do not hesitate to contact The Adoption Exchange for help, support, referrals, and to share successes. We look forward to hearing from you.

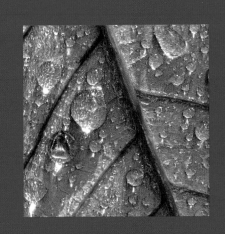

Thank You

We gratefully acknowledge our present and former Board of Directors, and the Advisory and Honorary Board Members for their underwriting support of this special project.

The Barnaby Family

Elaine Gantz-Berman & Steve Berman

Rick and Geraldine Brinneman

Brian, Chris, Jordan, Zackary and Jeff Corwin

Barbara Dalberg

The Englebrecht Family

Honey and Chuck Goldberg

Sherman Hamilton

The Jackson Family

What a joy it is to celebrate 25 years of The Adoption Exchange and those who have faithfully served our mission. Thank you for helping make wonderful memories for our children and their Forever Families. Nothing could be more important.
Pam and David Kiker and all of the Kiker Team

In honor of Colorado Human Services Workers who provide services to preserve, sustain and protect children and families.
Anonymous Board Member

Cynthia and Tyler Gambill

The Harris Family
Rich, Lisa, Zachary, Rachel and Olivia

With wishes for a future in which all children will be raised in loving homes.
Marlene, Ben, Paul & Aimie Krell Family

Susan and Tom Larkin and the Larkins blessed by adoption

*I'm proud to have been involved with The Adoption Exchange for twenty-five years
and to have seen the growth — the involvement of a variety of people and the children
The Adoption Exchange has helped to achieve permanent homes.
I hope to be involved just as long as I can make a contribution.*
Oneida Y. Little, Volunteer Child Advocate

Jim and Gerry MacDermott

Our sincere appreciation and congratulations on 25 years of truly caring . . .
Rich, Andrea and Luke Montoni

Brent and Marion Neiser

Founding Board of Directors 1982-1989
Sharon King Osborn

The Perlstein-Mizrachi Family

Ed and Mary Rand

Your tireless work makes the future so much brighter for so many children and families.
The Songer Family

Elaine Torres and Phil Workman

Larry and Judy Walker

Bert and Dixie van de Flier

David F. Zinger

Bibliography

Banks, Arta. *Wrong Feet First: A Gift of Stories for Your Inside Out Kind of Day.* Denver: Lovegifts Publishing, 2001.

Constello Consulting, Inc. *You Know You Are In A Permanent Home If* 2601 8th Avenue North, Great Falls, MT 59401.

Kavanaugh, James. *Faces in the City.* New York: E.P. Dutton & Co., Inc. 1972.

Sheehy, Gail. *Middletown America: One Town's Passage from Trauma to Hope.* New York: Random House, 2003.

Parker, Dorothy. *Solace.* LD, June 16, 1928.

Peck, Scott. *The Road Less Traveled.* New York: Simon & Schuster Adult Publishing Group, 1988.

Viorst, Judith. *Necessary Losses.* Simon & Schuster Adult Publishing Group, 1998.

Whitney, Diana and Amanda Trosten-Bloom. *The Power of Appreciative Inquiry: A Practical Guide to Positive Change.* San Francisco, California: Barrett-Koehler Publishers, Inc., 2003.

Whyte, David. *The Heart Aroused.* New York: Bantam Doubleday Dell Publishing Group, Inc., 1994.

Index